TEARS OF BLOOD

BY

MICHAEL SHERIDAN

First published in 2004 by

Mentor Books
43 Furze Road,
Sandyford Industrial Estate,
Dublin 18.
Republic of Ireland

Tel. +353 1 295 2112/3   Fax. +353 1 295 2114
e-mail: admin@mentorbooks.ie
www.mentorbooks.ie

A catalogue record for this book is available
from the British Library

ISBN: 1-84210-281-8

Cover by Graham Thew
Typesetting, editing, design
and layout by Mentor Books

Printed in Ireland by ColourBooks

CONTENTS

This book is dedicated to
the victims and their families
who suffer agonies that
no one should have to bear.

And to the power of good,
my mother Patsy,
surrogate mother Cissie Dooley
and her husband Maxi.

ACKNOWLEDGMENTS

My thanks to Danny McCarthy of Mentor Books for publishing *Tears of Blood*, to Una a patient and conscientious editor who could spot a mistake or contradiction a mile away, to Kathryn who succeeded in deciphering the hieroglyphics, to Nicola for the publicity and to all the crew at Mentor, including Fiona, Raechel and Edel.

Thanks also to Tara King for her research on the Galway chapters, and special thanks to all the families who spoke to me. And to Ger, Cian, Fionn, Sarah and Marty for their familial support as well as amanuensis Gerry O'Carroll, Kathleen, Mags and Ellie.

1
KILLING – THE AFTERMATH

Murder is defined as the unlawful intentional killing of one human being by another. Manslaughter is the unlawful but not deliberately planned killing of one human being by another. When a loved one is senselessly killed in a confrontation or row the surviving family members and friends experience anger, bitterness, remorse and guilt. All these feelings are intensified if the death is outside the strict category of accidental. Anger often turns to guilt as many relatives of victims believe that perhaps there was something they could have done to prevent the crime. In the circumstance of a trial the grief is revisited, often in the most upsetting manner, as the evidence is presented and witnesses cross-examined.

It is a traumatic period for all those involved. On the one hand, the family and relatives want to have the trial over as soon as possible to have closure, while on the other they want justice to be served properly. This, under our adversarial system of law, makes it very difficult as the defence team do everything in their power to mitigate the defendant's involvement.

The graphic evidence on the manner and cause of death, established and given by a pathologist, can be particularly upsetting. The pathologist is a vital part of murder and manslaughter investigations, and the expert evidence is given in a dispassionate and professional manner. But for the family or relative it is a grim reminder of exactly how their loved one died, which was often as a result of the most appalling and gratuitous violence. Many relatives have to leave court when the details are being presented.

In a recent case a Corkman, Keith O'Donovan (31), was tried for murder although he had pleaded guilty to manslaughter. He had stabbed twenty-eight-year-old Noel McCarthy in front of the victim's mother. The State Pathologist Dr Marie Cassidy gave evidence that the victim had died from massive internal bleeding and shock due to a stab wound in his left groin.

Dr Cassidy told the jury in the Central Criminal Court that, after conducting a postmortem examination on the deceased Noel McCarthy, she had found multiple injuries to the face, ear, groin and hand, as well as massive internal bleeding. She told the court that Mr McCarthy's femoral artery in his left groin was cut in two, resulting in '200ml of free blood in the abdomen and massive haemorrhaging around the kidneys and inside the pelvic area'. She noticed that he also had a stab wound to the bladder. There was a 5.6cm cut between his ear and mouth on the left side of his face, a slash wound that Mr McCarthy had received some hours before he was stabbed in the groin in an earlier incident in O'Donovan's house. Two superficial cuts were found on the back of his head and his ear, while a cut across the back of his hand 'was a typical site of a defensive injury'.

The evidence was too much for the victim's mother; Mrs Mary McCarthy left the court in tears.

It is beyond doubt that the evidence of the pathologist is hugely important in any murder, manslaughter or death under suspicious circumstances. For many relatives, despite the difficulties inherent in listening to that evidence in an open court, it is unequivocal proof of the brutality of the killers.

Many of these killers will make every effort to play down this brutality but the wounds to the body of the victim and the cause of death, when it can be established precisely, tell the real story of both their evil nature and their intentions. Relatives have said to me not to hold back on the details of the murders of their loved ones because these details give the most accurate portrait of the killers.

Media coverage, bringing the individual and unique tragedy into the public domain, results in further stress and pressure, and adds to the grief of the affected families. Since writing about the horrendous deaths of Veronica Guerin and Sophie Toscan du Plantier, as well as detailing the work of psycho and serial killers in Ireland in *Frozen Blood* and numerous other cases in *Irish Crime* magazine, the intensity of the suffering of families of loved ones who have died as a result of violence has made a deep impact on me.

The bare statistics in the media coverage is simply the tip

of the iceberg and such is the frustration of many families with their lowly place in the justice system that they have decided to voice their anger and disappointment with the legal system. Most people believe that what happens to us is linked to what we deserve. After a loved one is murdered or killed, the unfairness of it can be overwhelming and impossible to understand. We believe that when someone does something cruel or wrong, they should be punished quickly for it. When such retribution is not forthcoming, families and friends can feel frustrated, confused and let down.

The belief that the police are there to protect and the courts to punish is a basic tenet of society. If, following a murder or killing, neither the police nor the courts are able to do much to apprehend and punish the perpetrator, many core beliefs are shattered. As the families perceive it, the law bends over backwards to protect the rights of the perpetrators and rarely takes into consideration the lifetime of grief to which they have been condemned. People describe these feelings as secondary victimisation.

Normally, many of these families would try to deal with their individual tragedy and get on with their lives. But for the majority that is not possible. The killers rub salt in their wounds by invoking the appeal process, trying everything to get their sentences reduced. The families have been given life sentences, their loved ones will never be coming back, while the killers have under the justice system a finite time to spend in prison: the so-called mandatory sentence of life can mean anything but a lifetime in prison. There are very rare exceptions but the majority of killers can be walking the streets within eight years of committing the worst crime known to man – the taking of another human being's life.

The killers can then get on with their lives, however constrained the circumstances. Many families of victims find it almost impossible to do the same, such is the deep trauma they experience. There are some killers who express remorse for their actions but in the main they are exceptional; the majority show little humanity and no sense of sorrow even if they plead guilty. Owning up to the crime by giving a guilty plea is often self-serving to get a reduced sentence. This cold-hearted attitude drives another nail into the hearts of the families.

Much of the evidence gathered for this book on the effects of violent death on the families of victims is individual and statistically may be deemed anecdotal but there are common threads which unite the experience of families affected. Despite the huge increase in murder and manslaughter in this country, we have yet to make a proper study and analysis of the impact on victims' families.

There are, however, studies in the United States which are helpful in dealing with the phenomenon, bearing in mind that, in the US, mandatory sentencing is very strict: life means life. In lesser sentencing minimum terms are imposed, which, for killing, varies from twenty-five years upwards. Dean G. Kilpatrick, Ph.D and Heidi Reisnick, Ph.D of the National Crime Victims Research and Treatment Centre of the

Medical University of South Carolina have published impressive research on the subject.

Their research tells about the effects of murder on indirect victims. It finds that any type of unexpected death of a family member or friend produces negative emotions among survivors. There are several aspects of a homicide death that aggravate the survivor's emotional and behavioural reactions.

First, the victims tend to be younger than those who die of natural causes. Second, homicide death occurs unexpectedly, giving the survivor no time to prepare themselves for the occurrence. Third, the fact that death was produced by someone's intentional hate-filled act is difficult for family members to comprehend and understand. Fourth, there is a great likelihood that many survivors will have extensive and protracted involvement with the criminal justice system. Fifth, although this is not true in all cases, there is considerable stigma associated with homicide. Often, people blame homicide victims for doing something wrong which led to their being killed. Surviving relatives of those who have died of cancer or heart disease rarely have to deal with subtle accusations that the deceased was somehow responsible for causing their own death. On the other hand, people can be so horrified by the murder that they withdraw contact from those who have a family member murdered. Sixth, the crime of murder has always fascinated the public as well as the media. Therefore the families of victims are likely to see depictions of the crime repeatedly in the news media. This prevents them from grieving in private.

One national study in the United States of adults who had lost family members due to murder identified one in five as having developed post-traumatic stress disorder. Parents whose child had been murdered were two times more likely to develop this condition than parents whose child died as a result of accidental death or suicide. Sixty per cent of mothers and forty per cent of fathers developed symptoms of the disorder within four months of the deaths. For parents involved in the criminal justice process this figure jumped to seventy-one per cent. Those with the closest relationship to the victim (parents, spouses, siblings) were at the greatest risk.

Major depression is another side effect affecting up to half of the surviving family members.

A search for some type of meaning to the homicide death is common in almost all survivors. A study conducted seventeen years after the deaths found that ninety per cent of victims' relatives reported searching for a reason, some meaning, or other way to make sense of the death. They were still looking for answers even though it was several years after the event. For many, their basic views about life and the world had dramatically shifted.

The first reactions to the news of a death are usually shock, disbelief and numbness, even if the death is anticipated in some way. But when a loved one is killed violently by another person, the shock can be overwhelming and disorientating. Feelings of numbness are a normal way for nature to sedate a person to give them time to cope with the news of what has happened and can help relatives and friends through the early stages. The feeling of shock may last a few days, or even months, and the affected say to themselves 'I can't believe it' over and over again. They may feel they are in the middle of a nightmare from which they will waken to discover that the loved one has not really died, it was all just a bad dream.

After a sudden or violent death the 'normal' feelings of grief can be heightened and complicated by the practicalities associated with violent death. Because a trial is likely, there may be a delay before the person is buried and before the trial actually takes place. This means that the feelings experienced seem as though they will never go away.

As the shock wears off the relatives can be assaulted by very strong emotions. Breaking down and losing control, while disturbing to others, is a normal part of grieving. It is difficult for them to make sense of it all. Loved ones constantly question themselves about what happened before, during and after a murder. Since violence is the most common cause of death of people under the age of forty, parents suffer the added trauma of a perceived failure in protecting their child, leading to the unbearable reality of self-blame.

Those close to the victim long for them – to see, hear or touch them. They find themselves looking for the person and mistaking them for someone else in a crowded room or on the street. There can be a sense of expectation when the phone or the front doorbell rings. Parents may find that, years later, they once again experience feelings of loss, triggered by events such as when they see friends of their murdered child leave school or start a family – the ordinary milestones in everyone's life that have been denied to the parents of the murdered. Siblings can feel guilt for moving on with their lives, and miss the friendship and love of the departed.

Because someone has taken the life of a loved one, anger is a strong emotion in the family. The anger is directed towards the person who is arrested, the police and the justice system. The anger can be turned inwards or taken out on their nearest and dearest and may be so strong that those who harbour it fear that they are losing control.

After a murder any feeling of safety is shattered and the friends and relatives can worry for their own and others' wellbeing and safety. The perception is that danger is around every corner and can lead to panic attacks where the heart rate rises and breathing becomes laboured and difficult.

The loss of a special relationship leaves relatives feeling forlorn and empty. Sometimes they are avoided by friends who are afraid of saying or doing the wrong thing and feel that anything they do say will be hopelessly inadequate. On the other hand, those close to the victim can feel that nobody understands what they are going through and so they avoid contact. Shying away from people can store up trouble for the future and induce further loneliness and isolation. Being alone with their thoughts and feelings can be a frightening experience. The isolation can prolong grief and induce suicidal thoughts.

As well as the mental and emotional repercussions, the

aftermath of violent death can include a long and depressing list of physical reactions such as anxiety, sleeping difficulties, guardedness, nausea, forgetfulness and loss of appetite.

The upheaval can also lead to behaviour that is totally uncharacteristic. There may be a loss of calmness, ability to demonstrate affection and be infected with hate. Those affected may become irritable and difficult to deal with. The murder or killing, they feel, has changed their life forever. Added to this is financial strain, a further pressure that can be intolerable.

Many relatives of victims whom I have talked to have been permanently affected by the experience and, despite their determination to keep going, the negatives far outweigh the positives. Frustration with the legal system is a constant source of disillusionment and disappointment, intensified by the very real fear that the killers of their loved ones will someday be free to walk the streets of their neighbourhoods.

Under our system of law there is an uneasy line between the facts of the case, the rights of the victim and the perpetrator, the rights of the relatives of the victim, the rights of the investigators and the requirements of the judge in the matter of sentencing. In the arena of murder and killing the rules seem to be very unequal. All the more so, it might seem, in cases where the killer has not been brought to justice. The case of the murder of ten-year-old Bernadette Connolly in Collooney, Sligo in 1970 provides the classical example. Thirty-four years later, the surviving family of the victim are as traumatised today by the murder as if it happened yesterday. And as more recent cases prove, to name Lorraine O'Connor's murder as one tragic example, the pain and the loss of a loved one will never go away.

Increasingly, relatives of the victims of unlawful killing seek to have their voices heard in the public domain to shed the stigma that is attached to their position, and to express their pain in the most stressful fashion – by allowing the horrendous details of their loved one's deaths to be told.

Such courage demands not only adequate testament but also action in every sphere of a legal system that consigns the dead to the simple title of victim. They have been abandoned to the silence of the grave, but as long as their loved ones have a voice and the details of their killings are made public, the killers will never be forgotten.

Ireland, in modern times has become a killing field. By looking at historical and recent cases, both at home and abroad, this book will attempt to deal with some of the very painful issues thrown up by the unlawful taking of a human life.

2

THE VITAL ROLE OF THE STATE PATHOLOGIST

The State Pathologist plays a vital role in the investigation of murder, manslaughter and suspicious death. The body is considered a crime scene because vital evidence such as DNA in blood and semen can lead directly to the identification of the perpetrator of the crime. If there is a struggle then materials such as clothes fibres are exchanged between the killer and the victim and again these fibres which are collected at the scene, if matched, can help solve the crime.

The establishment of the cause and the time of death are two of the most important functions. After death the body goes through generally predictable phases of change which the pathologist tracks and observes. Death is primarily a cessation of bodily functions according to Dr Declan Gilsenan, a pathologist who has deputised for State Pathologists and who has many years experience of investigation of murder and suspicious deaths.

> It is a cessation of breathing, circulation of the blood and biochemical activity, the last two giving rise to observable phenomena. The end of circulation leads shortly to the sedimentation

of the blood to the lowest part of the body. For a body lying on its back it is to the back of the body. With a body on its left side it is to the left side. Because the weight of the body compresses those parts in firm contact with the surfaces, there are pale areas at these points.

A hanging or suspended body develops hypostasis [pooling of the blood] in the lower limbs, lower body and lower areas of the upper limbs. This usually appears half an hour after death and is at its maximum at about twelve hours after death.

Following death the muscles of the body are usually soft and limp for a period of between three and six hours. Then the muscles stiffen, most noticeably in the smaller muscles, gradually extending to the larger groups of muscles of the body. Rigor mortis, as this process is known, is usually at a maximum six to twelve hours after death. Rigor mortis continues for twenty to forty hours and then begins to recede.

Algor mortis, or postmortem cooling, still represents the most accurate method of estimating the postmortem interval in the first forty hours. Most methods assume the body is at the normal temperature of 37°C at the moment of death but this may not always be the case. If the person dies in freezing conditions or is suffering from a high fever, the starting temperature can be severely altered. Factors such as clothing, air temperature, air movement around the body can all influence the starting body temperature. After two or three hours the body cools at an average of 10°C per hour.

I once encountered a case in which the deceased was killed while immersed in a warm bath, then wrapped in a sleeping bag ready for disposal. The temperature of the body was in excess of the normal 37°C some hours after death. Bodies immersed in cold water do not follow the above rules due to direct conduction of heat away from the body into the water.

The stages of decomposition of the body can also provide clues to how long the victim has been dead. This is particularly useful if the body has been concealed for a number of days or more before discovery. For longer periods the level of infestation of the body by flies and maggots tells its own story of the length of time since death.

According to Dr Declan Gilsenan:

Postmortem putrefaction, or rotting, usually begins after three days with greenish discolouration of the lower wall of the abdomen. This purplish green colour spreads gradually over the body producing a marbling effect. Gas is formed in the tissues and causes swelling of the neck and face and bloating of the stomach. Foul-smelling liquid comes out of the body and any wounds present.

In the unusual circumstance where there is no blowfly [maggot] infestation, the tissues darken and dry, leading eventually to mummification. The variables that affect the rotting rate may include the surrounding heat, moisture and, most significantly, the presence of septicaemia [blood poisoning] in the deceased before death. I have seen a body eight hours after death with this condition present, displaying an appearance more appropriate to a body eight days after death.

The scientific evidence provided by the pathologist, whatever the variables in the circumstances of the individual case, provides anatomical detail that even within the inconsistencies of the system of law is rarely challenged.

In January 1996 the State Pathologist Dr John Harbison was at last given much needed help when a deputy was appointed. Harbison was at that time performing over 120 postmortems a year all over the country. It was an intolerable work load for a professional whose skill was vital, not only in determining the cause of deaths in general, but, most importantly, deaths under suspicious circumstances. Dr Marie Cassidy was born in Glasgow with the Irish connection of grandparents from Donegal. She was reared in the suburbs and describes her childhood as uneventful. Not born with a silver spoon in her mouth, her hard-working father ensured that his coal merchant business provided a very good education for the family.

Having completed her secondary school education Dr Cassidy studied medicine at Glasgow University from 1971 to 1978 when she graduated with an MBChB degree. She spent her internship in Lanarkshire in two country hospitals but readily admits that she did not like hospital life. She had no difficulty in working with patients but had some reservations about working with pompous doctors.

She began to specialise in pathology laboratory medicine and found it was an area of the profession that she both enjoyed and found challenging. In the mid-eighties she qualified as a forensic pathologist. 'Back then forensic pathology was considered the poor branch of the medical profession, and the profession considered forensic medicine to be second rate compared with general medicine,' she says.

It was just a year or two before the discovery of DNA fingerprinting by English scientist Dr Alec Jeffreys, a development which would catapult forensic medicine to the top echelons of the public consciousness. Cassidy stayed in that job for thirteen years and she became the first female full-time consultant in forensic medicine in the UK. For some years the police were wary of a woman in that position and were unsure of how to deal with her.

'You must remember that until recent years forensic

pathology was essentially a male preserve. In the early days the forensic pathologist tended to be put on a pedestal. The police tended to regard his evidence as being beyond dispute,' she says.

She had moved away from general pathology and truly found her niche. 'I think that most pathologists work towards practising in suspicious death cases and assisting State enquiries. It can yield very rewarding results. When you are involved in a specialist field like homicide you become concentrated, whereas in general pathology you are constantly moving from one case to the next,' she says.

Practising day to day in the State Pathologist's office, being called day and night to the scenes of bloody murder and decomposing corpses and being left with images that would test the strongest stomach and imagination, must be a huge strain.

'You have to be prepared to cope with all sorts of conditions. There would be no point in working in the job if you didn't think that you could follow it through. The practice makes a lot of demands on you both physically and mentally but it is rewarding to have delivered a thorough autopsy report which might help an investigation. When the day is done I get home as quickly as possible and relish the time that I spend with my family.'

The most distressing aspect of her job and also for the investigating team is when they have to deal with the death of children. On many occasions she has seen experienced gardaí reduced to tears in such circumstances.

'Nobody can prepare themselves for the shock of dealing with a mutilated body. It is a simple case: either deal with it or get another job,' she says.

When Dr Cassidy wakens each morning, she immediately switches on the radio to hear the news. The news indicates to her whether she might be travelling to some part of the country or simply going into the office.

Dr John Harbison retired in 2004 and Dr Marie Cassidy was appointed State Pathologist.

Layla Brennan: How forensics caught a killer

Layla Brennan, a young Dublin prostitute, got into a car at the invitation of a client one night and ended up dead, strangled by her own bra. Her body was dumped in a ditch in the Dublin mountains. In March 1999 her body was found, naked except for her bra around her neck and one shoe and one sock on her foot.

Her body had lain in the ditch for several days before gardaí and then Assistant State Pathologist Marie Cassidy supervised its removal. The victim had died of asphyxiation, and the neck and face were covered with scratches, consistent with a desperate struggle.

Layla Brennan (24) had been a dental receptionist in a practice near Thomas Street in Dublin but had become addicted to heroin and lost her job. She had, like a lot of female heroin addicts, turned to prostitution to pay for her chronic addiction. On the night she disappeared a twenty-seven-year-old Dublin man, Philip Colgan, had been drinking in the city centre. In Nassau Street he stopped his car to ask a woman for directions. Layla Brennan did not know it but she was in the wrong place at the wrong time and about to be caught in a cruel twist of fate. In turn she asked Colgan if he was looking for business. He opened the door, she got in and Colgan drove in the direction of Donnybrook. After parking in a secluded spot near Old Belvedere rugby club grounds, they each smoked a cigarette and she began to get undressed.

Colgan said he felt relaxed with Layla and changed his mind about having sex. But she was a heroin addict and desperate for the money for her next fix. She demanded the £60 that he had agreed to pay her. A disagreement followed and, according to Colgan, she said that she had his car registration. She had no idea that the man she was confronting was a violent double rapist. But addicts because of their condition do not possess the same sense of self-preservation as others might in that situation.

By pushing it she was signing her own death warrant. Despite his previous conviction for the double rape – he had served eight years for the aggravated rapes of a seventy-nine-year-old woman and a young Spanish student – Colgan was just a year free but had married and was apparently trying to live a respectable life. He believed he had a lot to lose if it was discovered that he had picked up a prostitute. In addition, the leopard does not change its spots; a man that is capable of raping an elderly woman and a young woman is essentially a very evil and out of control individual.

Colgan punched Layla to shut her up and when she began

to scream he started to strangle her until she lost consciousness. He then drove to Killakee forest where it is likely that he completed the strangulation with the straps of her bra. He dumped Layla Brennan's body in a ditch.

Such men are compulsive liars. They also have a compulsion to tell others about their crimes. In Colgan's case it was his wife to whom he spun a very strange tale. He admitted the killing but told her that he was homosexual and that his gay partner, a man called Wayne, had held him at knife point and forced him to carry out the murder. He said he had met the man in a gay bar before in Dublin and again on the night of the murder. They had oral sex and Wayne suggested that they pick up a woman. Wayne had sex with Layla and then held Colgan at knife point and forced him to commit the murder. Wayne was a tramp, he said, but at a later stage said that he had picked up a homeless man who was also present at the scene.

Colgan's wife rang the gardaí and he was arrested. He was first detained in the Central Mental Hospital in Dundrum and then placed in Mountjoy Prison where he concocted another tale to deflect blame from himself. But his self-delusion would be fruitless because forensics, unless improperly applied, do not lie. After a thorough search of the accused's home, gardaí found a bag containing the victim's clothes hidden in a shed and forensic tests confirmed that hair and blood consistent with the victim's types matched those found in the killer's car.

Mrs Colgan told gardaí that in the early hours of March 2

she got a phone call from her husband to collect him from St Anne's Park in Raheny. Colgan claimed that he had been beaten up by gardaí who had taken his car away from him. When she arrived, he was covered in mud and in a distressed and animalistic state. 'I'll remember that look until my dying day,' she said. 'He had the fear of God in him. His eyes were wild, absolutely terrified.' Colgan, despite his state, was weaving another fantasy version of events.

At his trial he went down another illusory path: he claimed that, although he had helped to move the victim's body, another unidentified man had killed her. This man was with him when they spotted Layla walking along Dame Street in Dublin. The man, he claimed, asked him to stop the car as he was owed money by Layla. Colgan asked if it was enough to pay for both of them. After parking near Old Belvedere rugby club, he got out of the car while the other man was having sex. When he returned between fifteen and thirty minutes later, he saw Layla lying face down in the back seat with a bra tied tightly around her neck. The men put the body into the boot of the car and drove to the Dublin mountains where they dumped it in a ditch. The other man struck the body with a wheel brace. Colgan got afraid and attacked the man, rendering him unconscious. He put the man in the boot of the car and then drove him further into the mountainous area and that was the last he saw of him. When Colgan was asked if the man was alive when he was put into the boot, he said he would rather not answer. Yet another fantasy story would be proved to have no foundation in fact.

His original statement of his sole involvement was far closer to the truth. In this statement he said that he had put his hands over Layla's mouth and grabbed her by the throat and squeezed. Dr Marie Cassidy's postmortem found that the victim had bruises around her face and injuries to her mouth and over her face which could have prevented her making any noise.

There were also definite signs of asphyxiation. These all provided a mirror image of the killer's original statement and proved that for once, he had been telling the truth. Allied with the forensic evidence found in his car and his shed linking him to the victim, there was more than adequate proof that no one but Colgan was responsible for the brutal killing.

On November 1 Philip Colgan was found guilty of the murder of Layla Brennan and given the mandatory life sentence by Mr Justice Paul Butler. The family of the deceased wept tears of relief as the unanimous verdict of the jury, who had been out for less than three hours, was read to the court. 'There is a God, there is a God,' one cried.

But without the forensics and in particular the vital evidence provided by then Assistant State Pathologist Marie Cassidy an evil man would have gone unpunished for the callous and brutal killing of a vulnerable young woman.

3
HISTORIC CASE – DEATH OF A DNA SCIENTIST

On April 7, 1984, English DNA scientist Helena Greenwood was alone in her residence in Walnut Avenue, Atherton, California. Roger Franklin her husband was in Washington, leaving her on her own for only the second time in five years, She was an executive in a biotech company and in an ideal position with her qualifications to exploit the next breakthrough in DNA technology.

That evening Helena, an ambitious and conscientious worker, went through work papers and scientific journals. As marketing director she was under a lot of pressure but could take it in her stride. Later she made herself dinner, watched television and went to bed early to read.

She fell asleep and some time later was woken by the frightening presence of a man in her room. His face was obscured by a hood pulled over his head and in his hands were what appeared to be a gun and a torch. She knelt bolt upright in the bed, clutching the sheets around her body.

The man told her to take off her clothes. She removed her T-shirt and her husband's boxer shorts. The man asked for money but his first request betrayed the real motive for his presence. Helena told him that he could have her purse which was in the study. He told her to get it.

As she walked naked through the house he followed her and watched while she emptied the contents on the floor. Showing no interest in the money, he was clearly excited by the sight of his victim being made even more vulnerable without clothes. He ordered Helena back to the bedroom. When they got there, he told her to switch the light on at the wall and sit at the side of the bed.

He put the gun in his pocket and moved towards her. He put his hands on her shoulders and she told him that she could not go through with what she thought was the ordeal of rape. He pushed her back towards the bed and told her that he was as scared as her.

The man then hurriedly pulled down his trousers, took out his penis and ordered her to put it in her mouth. Helena, complied, she had no choice. Quite quickly, the man pushed her head backwards and ejaculated over her face and the pillow beside her. He then pulled up his trousers, backed out of the room and warned her not to contact the police. She was frozen for a while and then rushed to the bathroom, immersed her face in water and brushed her teeth.

She dressed and ventured carefully out of the bathroom. She walked through the house, room by room, in fear and trepidation. In the kitchen she noticed that the sliding window over the sink was wide open. She went to the front door and opened it. Everything was eerily quiet. She ran to the next house and banged on the door but there was no answer.

The occupants of the third house she tried let her in and, after Helena had blurted out her story, they rang the police. She later made a statement to the investigating team after she had a sexual examination at the local hospital. She stayed with friends that night but went back to Walnut Avenue to collect documents and clothes. She rang a friend to come over to the house.

Her friend noticed a teapot on the deck outside and drew her attention to it. It had been removed from its usual spot. Helena rang the investigating team who collected it for forensic examination and fingerprinting analysis. This small piece of a crime jigsaw puzzle would in time prove crucial. Helena, reunited with Roger, put the awful experience behind her and buried herself in her work.

Married in England in 1973, the childhood sweethearts decided to pursue their careers in the United States where Helena could put her science doctorate to good use and where there would be ample opportunities for Roger's skill as a landscape architect. Here was a prudent, loving and ambitious couple with a long and fruitful horizon.

They chose the Bay area of San Francisco in which to live and Helena got a job in Palo Alto with Syva one of the leading firms in medical diagnostics while Roger completed his masters degree in the famous local university in Berkeley. After renting they bought a house in Walnut Drive in Atherton. They went on skiing and camping trips and developed a close circle of friends. They were going places and Helena switched from a scientific to a marketing role, one at which she excelled.

Helena did not tell either her family in England or her work colleagues about the sexual assault. It was a blot on the landscape of her life in California and she was not going to allow it to interfere with her work or any aspect of her life.

Meanwhile the investigating team under Detective Steve Chaput had meticulously preserved and examined evidence: the semen-soaked pillow case and the teapot which had yielded a complete print.

If the perpetrator was brought to court, visual identification would prove problematic because of his improvised disguise. As the discovery of DNA fingerprinting was still two years away, the semen sample would not play as important a role. The months passed by and no suspect was found.

But then there emerged a number of reports of an intruder breaking into apartments occupied by women. In one case the man told the two occupants that he had a gun. He wasn't going to rape them, but wanted them to perform oral sex on him. He ordered them to take their clothes off and he pulled out his penis but could not seem to get sexually aroused. When a third flatmate woke up and challenged him, the man, who wore a T-shirt over his head, fled.

The girls were able to give a good description of the intruder: athletic build, broad shoulders, long legs, well groomed with collar-length brown hair, smooth-shaven and tanned. There was another report of an aborted attack by a man of similar description. Steve Chaput as yet was unaware of these attacks, some aspects of which bore a close resemblance to Helena Greenwood's experience.

Meanwhile Helena had joined a new biotech outfit, Gen Probe. The job meant promotion, a seat on the board and more money, but she would have to relocate to San Diego. That would not be a problem. She would sell her Atherton home and finally leave all memory of her horrible experience behind her.

In early February 1985 in San Francisco at about 6 p.m. thirteen-year-old Chantal Clark looked up from the television to see a man in front of the window with his trousers open. He was masturbating. Chantal called the police and they arrived quickly. They spotted a man walking away from the location, gave chase and collared him. When they brought him back the teenager positively identified him.

He was brought back to the station for questioning and identified himself as Paul Frediani. He claimed that there was a mistake; he had been urinating, not masturbating. He was asked to explain a bottle found in his pocket. He said that it was hair conditioner, recommended by his hairdresser. The bottle, his trousers and a handkerchief were taken away for analysis.

The connection was made with the other incidents and while the girls were sure that the photo shown by police was the same man, not one of them could positively identify Frediani, who was at that stage living with his girlfriend, had a job and all the outward signs of respectability.

Meanwhile Roger had joined Helena in San Diego and they lived in a small, rented cottage in a village twenty miles outside the city. They loved the new location and started house hunting, eventually finding one for the not inconsiderable price tag of $500,000. But with the sale of the Atherton property plus Helena's salary, they could afford the repayments. The couple had a bright and affluent future as Gen Probe was in a very good position to take advantage of the explosion in DNA technology that would follow the 1986 discovery of DNA fingerprinting by Alec Jeffreys of Leicester University in England.

News of the breaks-ins and the masturbation incident involving Frediani eventually filtered through to Detective Steve Chaput who got a copy of his fingerprints and sent them to the lab for a comparison with the fingerprint found on the teapot. There was a match. The detective presented his case to the District Attorney and on April 19, 1985, a warrant for Frediani's arrest for burglary and the forced oral copulation of Helena Greenwood was issued.

Frediani was subsequently interrogated and saliva and head and pubic hair samples taken from him. A blood test was also taken and he was formally booked for the offence and locked in a cell to await the preliminary hearing before a judge who has to decide if there is a case to answer. It looked as if the gallop of a compulsive sex offender was about to be stopped. But justice often moves in very strange ways and in the case of Paul Frediani the trail to justice would prove to be a protracted journey, to and beyond the grave.

At the preliminary hearing in May 1985 Helena and her sexual predator were first brought face to face. While she could not provide a positive identification of her assailant, the judge ruled that there was sufficient cause for trial which was set for the following September. Frediani, for whom life was going very well apart from this glitch, was clearly shocked. While Helena Greenwood had a lot to lose by giving evidence, the accused had not only the possibility of his liberty but, at this juncture, his perceived reputation.

Just over three months later on August 22 Roger and Helena rose early as usual, had breakfast and at eight o'clock Roger headed off to work. Helena made a number of calls including one at 8.40 a.m. to an old friend. She had an appointment to keep in relation to the purchase of the new house and then she planned to go on to the office.

Helena Greenwood never kept the appointment and failed to turn up for work. The office rang the home phone but it just rang out. Then Roger was contacted and he drove back home. He tried to get in the gate but there was an obstacle behind it. Looking over the gate he saw that the object was the prone body of his wife. Helena was dead. He made his way to the house and rang 911.

Paramedics and detectives and crime-scene experts arrived in minutes and began the routine that is applied to every murder scene: the photographing of the scene and the body and the punctilious collection of evidence, which is placed in small bags and labelled.

The body was then removed to the coroner's office where a postmortem was performed the following day. One of Helena's fingernails was broken so it was clipped away for forensic examination in case a segment of her attacker's skin or blood might be trapped underneath.

The immediate cause of death was manual strangulation but the attack was savage, and defensive injuries on the body indicated that Helena had put up a fight before succumbing to a more powerful person. After the initial attack Helena's head had been bashed against the gate, probably while kneeling. Blood was then transferred to the attacker's hands and that blood was left on the victim's neck during the act of strangulation.

There were bruises on Helena's hands and face and cuts on her hands, evidence of her resistance to the attack. When she was finally beaten to the ground, her body should have remained flat on the ground. But there were two hand prints – in her own blood – on both ankles where the killer grabbed them, pushed up the knees and left her with her legs spread apart. This position was purposely arranged by the attacker, an act typical of sexual psychopaths.

But who would have wanted to kill Helena, not to mind position her body in a semi-sexual position? The person who had most to lose by her continued existence was Frediani because she was due to give evidence against him at his trial. He was already displaying the developing traits of a sexual psychopath, moving from a peeping Tom role to breaking into apartments occupied by women and attempting sexual assaults. The next rung on this rotten ladder is killing and in the case of Helena there was an extra incentive. It did not need rocket science to select the prime suspect. However, selection was one matter and evidence the next. This depraved act destroyed not only a lovely woman but also wreaked havoc on the minds of her husband and ailing father. Not for the first time, the killer murders more than the victim.

What Frediani did not anticipate was that, even in death, Helena Greenwood's evidence in the sexual assault trial was admissible. It would be read out by a third party, in the present tense, and the jury would not be made aware of the victim's death for fear of prejudice against the accused. After a delay, the trial commenced on October 14, 1985. The defendant appeared to reporters to have the stance of an arrogant man who found the proceedings somewhat boring.

The prosecution case was largely based on circumstantial evidence because the fingerprint was found on the teapot outside the house and scene of the crime, and the serological analysis of the semen, in the absence of DNA technology, could only narrow the secretor down to one in seven people. On the other hand, Frediani's alibi and explanation why his fingerprint happened to be on the teapot was weak and did not stand up to much scrutiny.

In the event the jury did not believe the accused's version of events and found Frediani guilty of burglary, forced oral copulation and possession of a firearm. The judge imposed a sentence of nine years. His lawyers soon lodged an appeal and he was let out on bail in February 1986.

Shortly after, his girlfriend made a complaint to the police that he had physically assaulted her and threatened to kill her. He had also been spotted by local patrols hanging around the streets in the early hours of the morning. It was clear to investigators that this man, despite the shock of the jail term and the effects on his personal life and his ability to make a living, had a sexual compulsion he could not control. He was caught prowling one night which resulted in his bail being revoked.

In January of the following year the appeal court overthrew the verdict: the sexual predator and prime suspect for the murder of Helena Greenwood was set to be released on the streets again. The furious prosecution team moved for a retrial which was set for July 27, 1987. With bail revoked, Frediani would remain in jail until the hearing. On July 29 there was a rerun of the original trial. The prosecution under DA Martin Murray succeeded despite a robust defence case. In less than four hours a different jury delivered the same verdict as their predecessors.

Frediani was back in jail and with good behaviour could look forward to being free again in two years. He was subsequently visited by two members of the murder investigation team. But the suspect was confident and was seemingly able to give a credible version of his movements on the day of the murder. Meanwhile his legal team were mounting a new appeal.

The wheels of justice were working very much in this sex

pervert's favour and seemed to have abandoned the murder victim and her family. This awful scenario was reinforced when the appeal court again ruled in favour of Frediani. There was now a prospect of a third trial. However both teams agreed a third trial was not a good idea and a bargain was struck. Frediani pleaded no contest to the burglary and sexual assault charges. This is an admission of guilt, carries a criminal conviction but cannot be pursued through the courts again. In return the gun charge was dropped and soon the perpetrator would be a free man again. Another slap in the face for Helena's husband and family, added to by the fact that the murder enquiry was getting nowhere. They were as much victims now as before. Meanwhile the perpetrator prepared for freedom.

But before he left prison, by law Frediani as a sexual offender had to give another blood sample, which for the moment mattered not a damn to him and was of little use to the murder investigation team. Although the offender's girlfriend had left with their two children, Frediani got a job and went to college at night to improve his CV. In contrast to his sexual compulsion, he led a very hard-working and disciplined regime, demonstrating the Jekyll and Hyde nature of his character.

He got on with his life and relationships with vigour and determination but men like him do not change. His anger, desire for control and perversion would let him down in a relationship, but in his work he would be known as a top-class employee, a friendly, funny and charming colleague with good social skills.

As the years passed the likelihood of catching Helena Greenwood's killer faded. It had become the classic cold case where the file had been left open but all hope of a result and arrest had evaporated. Unless one person had the time and a focused interest, the case would remain in the unsolved file. In the spring of 1998, that is exactly what happened.

Laura Helig a member of the San Diego County Sheriff's Department picked up the Greenwood file and read the investigators', crime scene and coroner's reports. She noticed that a sample of the victim's nails had been taken, logged and stored. Major breakthroughs in genetic fingerprinting had been made by now and, in January of the following year, the clippings and scrapings were sent to a private DNA lab for analysis. These procedures take time as the samples have to take their place in the queue of the busy serological institute.

Months later Laura Helig received a phone call to say that foreign DNA had been found on the fingernails. She was aware of Frediani being the prime suspect so the next step was to contact the State DNA lab to have Frediani's blood sample analysed and matched. The sample, which had been stored in a freezer for ten years, was sent to the private lab for analysis.

In November 1999 Laura Helig got the news that the DNA under Helena Greenwood's fingernails matched the blood sample taken from Paul Frediani. The District Attorney's office gave the go-ahead for further testing to solidify the forensic evidence. The net was closing in. The further tests proved conclusive. Laura Helig now had the case she had dreamed about.

An arrest warrant was prepared and Helig set about tracing the whereabouts of Frediani. It did not take her long to locate his address, car registration and driving licence number. In mid-December the arrest warrant arrived on her desk. The investigating team booked tickets for San Francisco for the following day and on the morning of December 15, 1999, Frediani was arrested while leaving his apartment for work.

Under questioning he remained composed and seemed distant and cold, denying any involvement in the murder. Frediani was then transferred to San Diego to await trial. Interviews with his friends and work colleagues confirmed he was a classic example of the Jekyll and Hyde syndrome; they could not believe that this charming individual was capable of such a brutal murder. Nothing in their experience of his character or behaviour suggested the slightest inclination to violence or sexual perversion.

The trial, after preliminary hearings and motions from the defence, got underway on January 11, 2001, with a further delay while the process of jury selection was undertaken. Five days later Paul Frediani was led into the courtroom to face the music he had avoided for almost sixteen years. A vigorous prosecution aided by the very technology that the victim held such high hopes for in her career convinced the jury. Frediani was convicted of first-degree murder.

In March 2001 he was sentenced. The judge described Helena Greenwood as perhaps the most blameless victim he had ever encountered in his court career. Since Frediani had shown no mercy to the victim, he said the court would show no mercy to him. He announced the verdict: life without the possibility of parole.

Justice, though a long time coming, was done for Helena Greenwood but it was too late for her husband and her father; the damage had been done many years before. Frediani would serve life in a prison, but he had a life, his victim was deprived of hers and by now her husband was dead and her father on the point of death. They were both destroyed by that awful act of August 1985.

Helena's husband Roger Franklin had addressed the court after Frediani was first found guilty of burglary and sexual assault and he spoke of the woman he loved and the dream that had been shattered. Helena, he said, was a very successful, career-minded professional woman who was driven by medical research. She was a cautious person who was not happy being alone and the effect of the assault on her was devastating. Every time she had to go on a trip, staying alone in a hotel was an ordeal. And the pyschological effects impacted on their relationship. It seemed to Roger that, because he travelled so rarely, the incident was entirely premeditated.

This was only the tip of the emotional iceberg. A year after the murder Sydney, Helena's father, visited his son-in law in California. Roger was depressed and planned to make a lone yacht trip around the world. Later he got on with his life and met another woman. He got married and became the father of two daughters. While it seemed that he had put the awful past behind him, Sydney believed that Roger never really recovered inwardly.

In 1999 Roger was diagnosed as having pancreatic cancer. It was in an advanced state and the prognosis was not good. He died almost six months later. His wife and former father-in-law believed that the trauma of Helena's murder had caused Roger's cancer and he died before justice at last began to knock on the door of the Greenwood murder.

At least Sydney had the satisfaction of hearing from Laura Helig that a man was to be arrested for the murder of his daughter, even at a time when he was himself dying from cancer. Yet he did not die happy because the death of a child is something from which a parent never recovers. The fact that a man took his only daughter away in a deliberate and merciless manner haunted Sydney, and until his dying day the anger and the anguish never abated.

For the relatives of the murdered it never does.

4
A YOUNG GIRL
IS MURDERED

In mid-April 1970 a huge drama was being played out in space. The third planned man mission to the moon, Apollo 13, was heading for disaster with mission control in NASA fighting to save the lives of the astronauts. It was a time when millions of people tuned to television coverage of space missions, the ultimate in man's search for adventure.

On April 11 the Apollo 13 countdown had taken place without major incident. Liftoff was at 2.13 p.m. and there was a hitch when the S11 stage's centre engine shut down two minutes early. An extra thirty-four second burn from the four outboard engines made up most of the difference but perhaps this was an omen of things to come. The planned velocity of the space ship was maintained and there was sufficient fuel left to boost the ship out of the earth's gravitational field.

Apart from what seemed a small problem, the first two days of the mission went according to plan. Fifty-five hours into the mission the crew began a television transmission from the command module Odyssey.

The crew described their temporary quarters and the interview ended on a light note when Astronaut James Lovell showed off a floating tape recorder playing musical selections that included 'Aquarius' from the musical *Hair* and the theme from Stanley Kubrick's film *2001: A Space Odyssey*.

The good cheer came to a sudden end a few minutes later when the warning system indicated low pressure in hydrogen tank 1. Mission control asked the crew to turn on fans and heaters. Ninety seconds after the fans were turned on mission control lost all electronic transmission for two seconds. The crew heard a loud bang and observed low voltage condition on an electrical conductor.

Astronaut Jack Swiggert reported: 'Okay Houston we've got a problem here.' But the full extent of the problem was not immediately apparent. The voltage recovered momentarily. The quantity gauge for oxygen tank 2 fluctuated and then returned to an off-scale high reading. There was repeated firing of thrusters. Within minutes the electrical output from fuel cells 1 and 3 dropped to zero. Mission control directed an emergency power-down of the command module.

There was pressure loss in oxygen tank 1 and, when checked, tank 2 was empty. As the pressure in 1 began to drop, Lovell and the crew abandoned the mission and sought safety and refuge on the lunar module. They did not know it then but the starting of the fans caused an electrical short circuit and the fan's motor wires caught fire. Though they burned slowly, the heat and the pressure soon ruptured oxygen tank 2. The escaping oxygen ignited and blew a panel off the ship.

The plight of the crew and the unfolding drama of the Apollo 13 mission was brought to millions all around the world. Apollo 13 looped around the moon on April 14 while the lunar module miraculously performed way beyond its two-day mission plan. As the module made its descent into the earth's atmosphere and was guided towards the planned splashdown in the Pacific Ocean, TV viewers all over the world held their breath.

In Collooney, County Sligo, a number of families were watching the final chapter of the Apollo 13 story unfold. In a nearby monastery, Cloonmahon, run by the Passionist order, the majority of the twenty-two members of the religious community were also glued to the Apollo saga. It was one of those events, like the murder of John F Kennedy, that concentrates people's attention and makes their memory very clear about the day. This phenomenon is known as the JFK syndrome.

But an event more catastrophic for the area than anything that might have happened to Apollo 13 was about to take place. As the splashdown neared one would have expected the memories of the locals to be razor sharp but for some inexplicable reason this did not happen.

Friday April 17 was a red-letter day in two different parts of the world.

In the townland of Doorla, near Collooney, Mrs Maureen Connolly telephoned a friend, Ellen Molloy, and asked her to buy some fish for the dinner and she would send her daughter over to collect it. Normally it was thirteen-year-old Ann

Connolly who did the shopping when required but her younger sister Bernadette had been at home sick with an upset stomach. Ann was the eldest of the four children, Bernadette (10), Tommy (9) and Patricia (4). Bernadette, a very lively girl, had recovered and was feeling a lot better. She wanted to fetch the messages from the Molloy house.

She got on her bicycle between 3.00 and 3.30 p.m. and headed towards the Molloy home which was only a mile and a half away in Lisaneena just off the main road. It began to rain heavily and Bernadette put the hood of her anorak over her head. A local boy Oliver Flynn and his mother Kathleen passed her along the way.

Over an hour later there was no sign of the little girl. Thirty-four years later in the living room of her house in Ballisodare in the company of her husband Gerry and sisters Patricia and Kerrie (who was born two years after the murder), Ann takes up the story:

> Being the eldest I was the one who used to go and get the groceries for Mum every day after school. That afternoon Bernie said she would go instead of me. She cycled off to collect haddock and potatoes. I got home at about 4.20 p.m. and Bernadette had not returned.
>
> My mother asked me to look for Bernadette. I got my bicycle and cycled over to Molloy's house. As I passed a ditch I noticed something shiny.
>
> I got to Molloys and some of the family were

watching the return of Apollo 13 on the television. When I was told that Bernadette was not there, I thought the Molloys were joking. When I realised that they were serious I became very worried.

I left the house with Tricia Molloy who was the same age as myself and we went back the route that Bernie would have taken. At the spot where I had seen the shiny object, we climbed over the ditch and there on the Lisaneena Road, just off the Boyle Road, we found my sister's bicycle. I instantly knew something awful had happened. It was like a sixth sense.

I found Bernadette's purse in a cow's hoof print. It was wet and the money was still in it.

After putting the bike against a tree the girls went back to the Connolly house. On the way they met Ann's father, Gerry, and told him about the discovery of the bike. He drove them back to the spot which was half a mile from the Molloy's house. When he got there he noticed two footprints in the mud – one large, that of a man and another small one, that of a child.

They returned to the house and Ann can recall her mother's cry of anguish. She put her hands on her head, howling and screaming, 'She's gone. Bernie's gone.'

My father then drove to Collooney Garda Station and reported Bernie missing. Sergeant Tom O'Brien took the details and a search was organised with local people, gardaí and members of the Cloonmahon community. That evening Superintendent Long from Sligo examined the spot where we had found the bike. By the following day there was still no sign of Bernadette. The family was deeply upset and were prescribed sedatives.

The family were being visited by the horrendous realities that come with the disappearance of a loved one: remorse, guilt, self-blame and the inevitable intrusive questioning that investigators have to follow in the course of their inquiries. Gerry Connolly would later be asked about his inclinations towards his own children. A horrendous experience for a great father and a man of total integrity whose daughter had disappeared.

Superintendent Long was convinced that the disappearance of Bernadette Connolly was one of abduction and possibly murder. He called for the assistance of the Murder Squad at Garda headquarters in Dublin.

When the team led by the hugely respected Detective Inspector Dan Murphy arrived, the search was extended and subaqua divers searched two lakes in the vicinity of where the bike was found. As the weekend passed without any finding, the family were in a state of deep shock and anxiety. 'It should have been me,' Ann said many years later to her sister Kerrie.

Gerry wondered whether he should have returned to Sligo from England where Bernadette was born. When he moved back with his wife and children from Birmingham it seemed like the right thing to do. It would have been entirely natural to suppose that the kids would be a lot safer in a lovely rural part of Ireland as opposed to the streets of a large English city. This was confirmed by the fact that there had been a child murder in Birmingham before the family left.

Gerry had warned the children about talking to strangers. The Connollys were decent hard-working folk who felt safe in their house surrounded by farmers and the community of Cloonmahon monastery. Gerry was a plumber by trade and was heavily involved in the other love of his life, the sporting games of the GAA. He was a very popular man in the area.

Ann was particularly close to Bernadette and they used to curl up together in bed at night. Even over three decades later the love for little Bernie shines through as the memories come flooding back.

> There was no cinema in our area then and so Bernie and I used to go to the Mary Healy School of Dancing, the youth club in Cloonmahon monastery and the Maria Goretti novenas. There was a little shop beside the church that sold medals and Bernie used to go in and collect them. She always had a scapular around her neck and medals pinned to her clothes.

The suffering of the family during those weeks of Bernie's disappearance was especially harsh due to a recent family tragedy. The previous October Maureen Connolly had given birth to a baby boy, Gerard.

> Little Gerry died in hospital ten days later and I remember that the way she was told of the death was appalling. Mum was so exhausted from staying up with him in the hospital that she went back home for a night. Before she went to bed she decided to ring to see how he was. In the most matter of fact, unsympathetic manner the nurse told her that he had died.
>
> The shock nearly killed her, the baby had been dead for two hours and nobody had bothered to ring and tell the mother, even though we were only one of two families in Doorla who had a phone. That was only six months before Bernie disappeared, not even enough time to get over grieving for her dead son.

The investigation team had established that fourteen people had been on the same route as Bernadette on April 17, yet only two had made a positive sighting of the young girl.

Detective Inspector Murphy ordered a re-enactment of Bernadette's journey, utilising her sister Ann. This established that she reached the entrance to Cloonmahon monastery four minutes after leaving her house. She could have passed three men working in the area but they denied seeing her. There later emerged good reasons for their denial: they were on a stealing expedition. One way or another they were not saying anything.

This marked the beginning of a wall of silence. Statement and counter statement would frustrate the investigation of the disappearance of the young girl and haunt the family until this day. It would also haunt the chief investigator Dan Murphy until his dying day. There was a fingerprint found on the bike, but this would lead down a blind alley. There was another lead that seemed more promising: four witnesses saw a green van in the area around the time of the disappearance of the young girl.

The Passionist order in Cloonmahon owned a green van and the team focused on its whereabouts on April 17. It was discovered that it could not be accounted for between the crucial early hours of Bernadette's disappearance and the time it was returned by a member of the community just before eight o'clock that evening. Further investigation revealed that a petrol station attendant James McTiernan said that the same van driven by Brother X pulled into the station between 7 p.m and 8 p.m. on the same day.

His memory was clear, he said, because the event occurred as the Apollo 13 team were coming out of the lunar module after splashdown in the Pacific ocean.

The cleric subsequently denied that he was there at that time and day. He claimed it was the previous day, but the attendant was insistent and clear about his memory. Obviously, there was something very suspicious about this incident and something equally suspicious about the behaviour of another member of the monastic community, Father Columba, who had literally moved into the Connolly family home to apparently offer the stricken members moral support in the darkest hour of their existence.

Letters of sympathy were being sent to the Connollys from all over the country. Columba collected the post and delivered it to the family. He opened most of the letters and the family later believed that he pocketed many that might have reflected badly on the monastery.

Ostensibly he seemed to be playing the role of pillar of support and comfort but in reality both the family and the investigating team were deeply suspicious about his role and his motive. DI Dan Murphy considered him to be a suspect in the abduction of Bernadette and both Gerry and his daughter Ann did not trust him.

Ann recalls,

> While all this mayhem was going on around us, Father Columba moved into the house with us. Even when everyone else was gone, he stayed in our tiny two-bedroomed house. Looking back now it seems abnormal that someone would stay in such a small space for so long. I remember that even though I thought it strange, when I asked about it everyone said, 'It's to support your Dad.'

But Gerry felt, as his eldest daughter did, that Columba was at turns both dominating and devious. He was feeding them bits of information, one piece in particular that was, in retrospect, ominous. He told them that one night he had driven to the house and he saw a strange car parked outside which drove off as he approached. He followed the car but later lost it just as they reached a corner near Boyle. Columba's description of the location would prove to be just yards away from the spot where the body of Bernadette Connolly would shortly be found. Was he deliberately leading the investigation to that spot?

As far as Ann Connolly is concerned the member of the monastic community was signalling he had knowledge of the crime. In a manner common to many killers he revealed information in an attempt to deflect attention from his own involvement. However, in many cases this can lead to a conviction just as Ian Huntley asking the police if they had found the clothes of Holly and Jessica did. The police had not released the information that the two little bodies were found naked. But in Bernadette's case, Columba's revelation led nowhere because, despite Dan Murphy's suspicions and request, Columba would never be brought in for questioning.

At this stage the investigation was still technically a missing persons inquiry – until August 4 when Mrs Margaret O'Connor got a very bad smell when she was working on a bog at Limnagh near Boyle. Down in a drain near the spot she came across skeletal remains. The teeth suggested to her that they were not those of an animal. She told her husband and subsequently they reported the find to the local gardaí.

When they arrived they found that there were three

miraculous medals on the vest attached to the remains. Ann
Connolly had already told investigators that her younger
sister had a habit of doing this and it immediately became
obvious that the body of the decomposed child was indeed
Bernadette Connolly. It was confirmation of a fact that
everyone feared. The location was fifteen miles from where
the victim's bicycle was found. Both Dan Murphy and other
investigators subsequently suspected that the body may have
been firstly concealed close to the site of the abduction and
then later moved.

The examination of the body by Assistant State Pathologist
Dr O'Neill confirmed that the size and bone structure of the
body was that of a girl of Bernadette's age. Both legs and the
right arm were missing as were some of Bernadette's clothes
including her underwear and shoes. Her glasses and a signet
ring were also gone. Despite the state of decomposition of the
body it was found that the young child had been raped and
strangled. For some reason this was not revealed to the family
who were told, when questioning how Bernadette died, that
they were better off not knowing.

It has been proved that the relatives of murder victims deal
better with their grief by knowing details that confirm the
monstrous nature of the killer. But this was 1970 when
murder was rare, the so-called olden days when investigators
understandably believed in sparing the relatives by not
revealing the gory details of their loved ones' deaths. But
other truths which even then were important to the Connolly
family were, by dint of silence and possible cover-up, denied

to them.

While the confirmation of the crime shocked the local community, there were witnesses from that community who proved to be unforthcoming with the truth. For some reason their cooperation, which could have led to the truth about the death of an innocent was not given.

While such a lack of commitment and cooperation in a rural community, so redolently dealt with by John B Keane in his play *The Field*, may be deemed to remain a mystery, when analysed coldly goes beyond the reality of the unexplained. Not so much a mystery as a cover-up, the very opposite of the simultaneous event – the Apollo 13 near disaster. This event was thoroughly analysed in the aftermath with reasons given and blame apportioned. That was not to be in the case of the callous and brutal murder of Bernadette Connolly. The most likely source of the cover-up was from certain members of the Cloonmahon monastery. Meanwhile in the outside world, witnesses would offer a maze of contradictory statements.

On August 24 Sergeant Tim O'Brien was involved in a casual conversation with a man from the village who, talking about the subject of fingerprinting, claimed that anyone's prints could have been on the bike including his own. He explained that he once put the bike into the back of his car. He was subsequently asked for his fingerprints. The technical experts compared them to the print on the bike and got a match.

It seemed to the investigators to provide a lead but it ultimately finished up in a dead end when the man was able to provide a solid alibi and satisfactory evidence that he was nowhere near the site of the abduction on the day.

Witnesses were re-interviewed as the team trawled through statements. Two witnesses who were in the area on the day gave information that they had not revealed first time round. They had seen a van parked at around 5 p.m. at the location where Bernadette's body was found. One of the men later told a friend that it was the monastery van. The friend informed the investigation team of the conversation. It became abundantly clear to the senior officers that getting accurate information from the witnesses was like extracting teeth with a pliers.

There were reports of other conversations connected with the green van but when members of the team followed them up the people who were supposed to have seen the van denied any knowledge. One man was confronted with the men with whom he had spoken about the van but, while he admitted a conversation had taken place, he said he had made no mention of the green van.

The investigation team were convinced that these men knew more than they were willing to divulge but they could not be budged on what was the major lead in the murder hunt. The information would have led to intense investigation within the monastery and the interrogation of two clerics, including Brother Columba. The reason for the reluctance of witnesses in regard to the van can only be speculated upon but the implications were enormous.

This was a time in Ireland when the Church was the

ascendancy, all powerful and immune to the sort of investigation that could expose the massive scale of cruelty and sexual abuse carried out by the clergy. One can only imagine the fallout had a member of the Cloonmahon Passionist community been brought to Collooney Garda station for questioning in relation to the abduction and murder of a young girl who was wearing three miraculous medals on her vest.

The witnesses were convinced that, however reprehensible their reluctance, with the notable exception of the petrol station attendant, no one would believe their word against a cleric and that if they stood their ground there could well be repercussions. There is little doubt that the Church would not stand idly by in this dangerous circumstance when already it had managed to hide widespread abuse, and even deaths, in institutions. There is also no doubt that if a local lay person was the focus of the investigation, the witnesses would perceive they had less to lose by being truthful.

Dan Murphy and his team were facing huge obstacles; they might as well have been in Russia investigating the connection between a KGB agent and a murder. Thirty years on they would have had the benefit of a disgraced Church, DNA fingerprinting and psychological profiling. This last has found that many killers place themselves at the centre of the action, befriending the family of the victim, and giving interviews.

That is exactly what Father Columba was doing in a most calculated and cruel fashion, and was entirely self-serving, giving the impression that Cloonmahon really c

On another level, it was highly manipulative: th
presence right at the centre of the murdered girl's
would give the impression that the Connollys were close
the community and trusted its members.

This would further inhibit witnesses who saw the green
van. They did not know that in fact the family were highly
suspicious of Columba's gross invasion of their privacy in the
midst of appalling grief with Bernadette's mother Maureen
immobile and lying in bed in the grip of sedatives.

The significance of the cleric's behaviour could not have
escaped the attention of a wily and experienced murder
investigator like Dan Murphy. There were, as in all murder
investigations, subplots and other coincidences which required
the attention of the team. Two men had been in the area at the
time of the murder, one Scottish and the other English, both
of whom had a history of sexual offences against children. The
Englishman, Bob Reynolds, was questioned three years after
the murder when he was arrested in 1973 in Castlebar for the
abduction and rape of a girl just one year younger than
Bernadette. He received a paltry six-year sentence.

He was ruled out of the frame for Bernadette's death when
he could not be placed in the Collooney area at the vital time.
The Scottish man was, in their view, a more likely candidate.
There was a sighting of him in the area by a young boy who
claimed he lunged at him from a vehicle. He memorised the
registration number of the vehicle but never passed on the
information at the time because his father told him not to.

Scottish man who had worked in
…evision repair man was traced by
…ed but, then in his seventies, said
…le of the time.

1984, Dan Murphy believed that
…as posted to Botswana in the
… murder, was responsible for the
…………………… …irl which destroyed the Connolly
family. At the time of the murder inquiry Dan Murphy,
universally admired for his skills of detection and
investigation, wanted to bring in Columba for questioning.
He was prevented from doing this by senior officials.

His investigation of the happenings in Cloonmahon
monastery on the day of the murder was hampered by totally
conflicting accounts of members' whereabouts. One
statement said that Columba was missing at the vital time,
another that he was watching the Apollo splashdown, and a
third that he was asleep in bed. There was general agreement
that the van was missing at the time. This alone is not
indicative of a cover-up, but why was Dan Murphy prevented
from bringing in Columba and how, as *Evening Herald*
journalist Stephen Rae in his account of the case in *Guilty:
Violent Crimes in Ireland* revealed, did a highly confidential
report on the investigation end up in the possession of the
Irish clergy.

The report read:

> At the time the bulk of the investigation team's
> suspicions still surrounded the monastery van.

One of the senior gardaí at the time reported to his authorities: 'A certain amount of suspicion lay on the Cloonmahon van, which is a dark green Ford Escort. The van was not satisfactorily accounted for during the period 4.30 p.m. to 7.55 p.m. Since the investigation resumed, suspicion has hardened towards the monastery van having been on the Lisaneena road on that afternoon.

'We are not entirely happy about the Cloonmahon monastery van. However, in the absence of more tangible evidence, there is little that can be done, irrespective of what our feelings are.'

As soon as his report arrived in headquarters, the investigation team was asked for a second copy. Somehow this copy ended up in the hands of members of the Irish clergy.

This proves that there was collusion at the very highest level of the Garda authorities with the Irish clergy who, incidentally, passed on the report to the Passionist Fathers (They held the chaplaincy to the Garda Síochána at that time). It would not be outrageous to suggest in the light of this revelation that even more detailed information from the investigation was leaked.

Sunday Independent journalist Brighid McLaughlin worked on the case for three years and interviewed both

Brother X, who James McTiernan said was driving the van, and Father Columba. She tracked Columba down while he was home from Botswana for a retreat. When she mentioned the murder, 'he went aspirin white and told me he couldn't remember where he was on the night of the murder or whether he had his fingerprints taken. He said he had been in the van earlier.'

He then concocted what can only be described as an outrageous theory on who was responsible for murdering Bernadette.

> It is my deepest feeling that it was the security forces who abducted, raped and murdered her. I heard that there was a consignment of IRA guns coming into the Collooney area around the time she disappeared.

Brighid's interview with Brother X is a bit more revealing:

> He told me that the gardaí were very tough on him. They dug up the manure pit and the monastery's septic tank. They took his fingerprints twice. When I asked Brother X for the fifth time was he at the petrol station, his answer knocked me for six.
>
> 'It may have been me,' he said.
>
> There was a sharp intake of breath on my part. Brother X was angry. 'I don't want to hear or talk about it.'
>
> When I asked him why he lied to the

investigation squad, he said the following:
'I didn't lie in a sense. I didn't know what time it
was. I had nothing to do with Bernadette
Connolly's murder. I was at the petrol station
just getting petrol.

'Are you saying that Mr McTiernan was
telling a lie?'

'I'm saying that Mr McTiernan was wrong.
I differ with him on times.'

'Do you believe that Father Columba Kelly
was involved?'

'I don't know that he didn't do it, but I don't
believe he did. Goodbye.'

There are a number of strange things about the replies of
Father Columba, who died in Botswana in 2001, and Brother
X. Columba admits to having been in the van and his cock-
and-bull IRA story is so far off the mark as to be a suspicious
invention. Also it is extraordinary not to remember whether
his fingerprints were taken.

Brother X for the first time reveals that he was the driver
of the green van identified by James McTiernan and
contradicts the statement he made thirty-two years before to
the murder investigation team. In that statement he insisted
that he had pulled into the station the day before the murder.
There had never been any suggestion that he was the killer, so
why would he lie?

But that is exactly what he did and he admits that James

McTiernan was correct. He also admits that he did not know what time it was when he was at the station. But then he contradicts himself when trying to explain away the lie by saying that he differed with the station attendant on the matter of time. How could he when he said he did not know the time?

His reply to Brighid's question about the possibility of Columba's involvement is most extraordinary. That statement coming from a member of the Cloonmahon community who was at the monastery on April 17, clearly shows there was a doubt in his mind and this doubt allows for the possibility that Father Columba could have done it.

He then quickly terminated the conversation in a manner that suggested that he felt he had already said too much. Like some other witnesses in this inquiry it seems that the cleric knew more than he was prepared to divulge and like others actually lied when confronted by investigators. Those lies all related to the most relevant and vital clue in solving this brutal and appalling murder of an innocent girl – the green van belonging to the monastery.

Meanwhile the family suffered on without the consolation of a real breakthrough in the murder investigation. The passage of time has not healed the open wound at the heart of the Connolly family.

'My poor father and mother were worn out by the death of Bernadette. They lived and died broken people. To me, my father and mother and Bernie have not been laid to rest,' says Ann.

The youngest sister Kerrie was born after the murder but suffers along with her two other sisters.

> I have spent my life looking at Bernie's photograph on the mantelpiece, wondering what she was like and what happened to her. I watched my parents fall apart and eventually die of grief. I was ten years of age when Mum died of cancer and I cannot remember a time that she wasn't sick in hospital. Every day I saw the pain in my mum and dad's faces. I am pregnant with my first child and I dread what the effect of Bernie's death will have on my attitude to my child and the thought that anything similar could ever happen again.

Patricia was four years old at the time of the murder and like her sister did not escape the trauma.

> I used to find Mum crying in the kitchen and saying Bernie would have loved this or Bernie would have loved that. Mum had cancer three years before she died. When she was dying in hospital people could hear her calling Bernie's name over and over again. Then Dad died on December 28, 1999. The four of them are buried together, Mum, Dad, baby Gerry and Bernie.

Ann and her husband Gerry and her sisters believe that even after such a length of time there should be a proper reinvestigation of the murder. There are a number of questions they want answered about the original investigation which, they contend, was stunted and interfered with because the prime suspect and the vehicle thought to have been used in the abduction and murder was from the Cloonmahon monastery.

'I can't bear to think of Bernie being abducted and what happened afterwards,' says Ann. 'How can I meet her on Judgement Day and say "Bernie, I did nothing. I let them away with your murder." I can't and won't let her down.'

The family say that over much of the past three decades they have never had communication from the gardaí about the murder investigation. Two years ago the family wrote down their questions. Ann Connolly explains:

> During the thirty-two years since the murder, and particularly the last four of that period, references to our family and aspects of Bernadette's disappearance have been discussed in the media. Media people and researchers are contacting our family about the failure of the investigation and aspects of the case previously unknown to us.
>
> This is not just a case to our family. This is about a member of the family who was very cruelly taken from us. A very emotional subject and a lifetime of pain. We want a reinvestigation. We ask a few questions that we feel are both pertinent and important.

We believe that the case is still open. We would like to know who is heading the investigation and if it would be possible to get in touch with that person.

We want to know why statements were allowed to be changed.

We have heard that a man told two neighbours that he saw the green van stopping where Bernadette's bike was found. Was a statement taken from him? If so, was he allowed to change it? Was this source the first information that placed the green van? Was there anyone else able to put the green van at the location? Was the original witness questioned recently?

We have heard that Brother X said that he gave two sets of fingerprints and that Father Columba Kelly has said that he could not recollect giving any. Could this be explained? When was Brother X last questioned?

We believe that an important report on the investigation which centred on the green van was copied and passed on to the clergy by the Garda authorities. The implications of this action are highly compromising. How and why did this happen?

Who was the prime suspect whom Dan Murphy wanted to arrest before he died? What evidence did he have? Was it followed up after his death?

When was the case last investigated? Do you have any other leads to follow?

What are the guidelines on the burial of the victim of an unsolved murder? Would her clothes hold any forensic evidence? Have the clothes, medals and the bike been kept in storage?

Was the green van searched for trace evidence, that if it was involved would have contained fibres from Bernadette's clothes or other forensic evidence had she been assaulted in the van?

It has been suggested by the media that the investigation has been a failure. Has it been or what has been done in the interim?

The family subsequently met a representative of the Garda authorities and put those questions to him. They found the answers unsatisfactory in many regards. They were told that Columba must have had his fingerprints taken, the van must have been searched. The Connollys felt that this was all very vague. When it came to the physical evidence, the representative assumed it was in storage but could not say where.

The Garda representative was to come back to them, but they have heard nothing and are fearful that the physical evidence may be lost. If searched, the green van must have yielded evidence. Where is it, they ask. They also point out the fact that the glasses that Bernie wore were never found.

Kerrie also says,

> The gardaí could not tell us whether Bernie was buried with her clothes on or not. She wasn't, but if she had been, it would have been disastrous from the point of view of evidence. But they didn't know then and they don't know where the clothes are to this day.

Subsequently a high ranking Garda officer visited Ann Connolly's house and was very nice and respectful, however the family say that they were no wiser after the visit and have not heard from the gardaí since.

A retired member of the Murder Squad who worked under Dan Murphy on a number of other murder investigations says that he was a superb policeman who would leave no stone unturned to track down a killer and who also had an unerring instinct in the earlier part of an investigation for the direction in which it was going and to whom it was leading. That being the case, if Dan Murphy wanted to bring in Father Columba for questioning he had very good reason for doing so. A member of the investigation team at the time confirmed this to the Connolly family.

> Dan Murphy definitely wanted to arrest Father Columba and bring him in for questioning in relation to the abduction and murder of

Bernadette Connolly and to account for his movements on the day. As for the green van, it was the only vehicle in the frame and was seen on the day by a number of witnesses.

Unfortunately the powers at the top of the Garda tree had agendas other than justice and the obvious and appalling facts of the murder were not going to interfere with political expediency. After the investigation file was leaked, Dan Murphy and his team were 'sent to Coventry' by members of the Passionists.

Highly ironic when it looks like a member of that order got away with murder.

There were fourteen people on the route that Bernadette Connolly took on that fateful day. It is beyond any doubt that one, two or a number of them saw a vehicle on the road. One man was driving his tractor up and down the road and spotted the green van at the ditch where Bernadette's bike was found.

The only other vehicle was that driven by the Scottish repair man and that was only seen by a young boy on a bike.

The last twist in this horrendous saga involves a deathbed confession of a local man who was working along the route that Bernadette took but, for his own reasons, kept his silence. On April 17, 1970, he saw the green monastery van parked opposite a ditch. A man was lifting a child's bicycle from the side of the road and putting it over the ditch, clearly in an effort to conceal it.

That man, he said, was Father Columba.

5

DEATH OF A CABBIE

A lot can be told about the mind of the killer from the details of the postmortem, evidence from the crime scene and the statements made by the killer while in custody. Other conclusions can, as in the case of psychopaths, be drawn from past history and the personal and environmental factors in the upbringing of the killer.

For many years psychologists and forensic psychiatrists have studied murder cases and interviewed the perpetrators in an effort to discover where the urge to kill comes from and why it takes over to the extent of sweeping away inhibitions and the natural fear of having to pay for the consequences. Is a killer born or made? Is there a genetic predisposition or is it due to social conditioning?

It is quite clear that the potential to kill is in all of us but the vast majority do not exercise this option even in the most provocative of circumstances. For many of us those circumstances simply do not arise. But at some stage throughout our lifetime some of us will harbour a murderous thought. This may be against a person who has done what we perceive to be a terrible wrong, depriving us of something very valuable whether it be money, a house, a prized possession or, terrifyingly, a lover, friend or spouse. Somehow most of us baulk at acting on the thought, reasoning that we would have a lot more to lose facing the consequences of that action. This even in a country whose system allows too many killers to literally get away with murder.

But others are less concerned with what will happen if they kill. The increase in murder in this country is quite staggering. Open a national newspaper almost any day of the week and there will be the report of a killing or murder or, if not, a report of a court case resulting from murder or manslaughter.

As many of the cases in this book demonstrate, the idea a killer is in some way insane is hardly ever true. The perpetrators try to somehow diminish the responsibility for their actions by lying about the circumstances, blaming drink or some sort of temporary insanity.

International studies have proved there is another explanation: the killers are rational, calculating and, as serial killer Denis Nielsen explained, 'The mind can be evil without being abnormal.'

The word evil has a dramatic connotation but the definition is more simple and fits the minds of the majority of killers like a glove: a force or power that brings about wickedness or harm.

If we can never completely get into the mind of a killer, a lot can be told by the method of murder.

Murder, by definition, says that the killer intended to carry out the crime. A murderer is categorised as an organised killer if he will not attack until he is in complete control of the location and situation. The control may be achieved by the use of ropes or a ligature and the perpetrator likes the killing to be slow and deliberate.

The method of killing is hands-on with the victim being stabbed or strangled. This allows the killer a personal and close method of murder with the feeling that he is the master of the situation. The attack is often sexually motivated. This organised killer has a background of violence and sexual assault and often consumes alcohol or drugs in advance of the murder.

The organised killer likes to return to the scene of the crime, be around when the body of the victim is discovered, keep trophies of the murder (taken from the victim) and participate in the investigation.

The return to the scene of the crime is to fuel the memory and fantasy of the killing, and the pleasure that is attached to it. Being present when the body of the victim is discovered is motivated by the feeling of power and control it gives.

The trophies taken from the victim can be jewellery, clothes or underwear, and are utilised to relive the murder fantasy and achieve sexual pleasure. The killer will often wear the clothes and underwear for the purpose of masturbation.

While being involved in some way in the murder investigation is highly risky, it puts the killer on a high and gets him attention which he craves.

The calm organised aura of the killer changes when he is caught, and he may adopt the personality of a mad man pretending that he was told to commit the murder by voices inside his head. He may also blame the consumption of alcohol or drugs, or use the excuse of a blackout during which he remembers nothing of his actions.

Investigators confronted by this apparently bizarre behaviour know only too well that it is a smoke screen created to give the impression that the killer's faculties were somewhat diminished at the time of the crime. They are aware that this is a strategy to reduce responsibility, and is aided by a tendency to lie about the details and motivation of the crime, not only in statements to investigators but also in court evidence.

The killer will stick to his manufactured version of the crime even when confronted with incontrovertible forensic evidence. The purpose is to deflect from the often horrific method of murder and to plead the lesser charge of manslaughter. Again, even while found guilty of the primary charge, the killer will stick doggedly to his version, hoping that it will be taken into account if the matter of parole arises.

The other category of killer comes under the heading of disorganised and will choose the victim at random. The murder takes place on a whim with the primary motive being simply to kill. He has had, generally, no previous contact with the victim and his method of killing does not include rape or torture but is carried out in a state of frenzy with a high degree of violence.

Such is the degree of frenzy, the killer does not care about leaving evidence at the scene of the crime; he is like a vampire with an overwhelming lust for blood. Perverted, violent or sexual thoughts will be left to be carried out on the corpse of the victim. These acts may include anal and vaginal intercourse, and mutilation of the breasts or vagina with bottles, sticks or knives. Souvenirs are also taken: clothes, underwear, even body parts of the victim.

These killers are loners who have a grudge against society, and in particular women, and are motivated by a desire for revenge against society. The victim of the murder comes to represent all that the killer hates and he sees the victim not as human but as an object.

These loners are often sexually inadequate, incapable of sustaining a relationship and get their sexual thrill by means of violence and having sex with a corpse that cannot experience or criticise the sexual dysfunction.

As a child, the disorganised killer may be exposed to an uncommunicative father who enforces harsh discipline, causing the child to be withdrawn, a silent type who internalises the hurt and the pain which festers as anger against the world. The child has a low IQ and performs badly at school. This fosters further resentment as he falls behind his classmates and feels inferior to other people.

Classically the violent inclination of disorganised killers starts with cruelty to animals which they kill as a prelude to attacking people when their anger and inadequacy explodes in an orgy of violence.

It happened seven years ago but to this day, even the most

seasoned of gardaí feel sickened by the recollection of the horrific murder of the popular Galway taxi driver, Eileen Costello O'Shaughnessy. The forty-seven-year-old separated mother of two was viciously beaten to a pulp after she innocently transported her murderer to a quiet, isolated laneway in Claregalway on the cold winter's night of November 30, 1997. Her lifeless body was then dragged further along the muddy boreen and dumped near a gate. As light broke the following morning a local farmer made the grisly discovery as he attended to routine chores on his farm.

The lovable mother of two was a bloody, crumpled mass, every dignity in life robbed in death.

On the previous evening suspicions were aroused after Eileen failed to turn up at her taxi firm depot for the 9 p.m. handover. An hour before she had radioed to say that she had picked up a fare in Eyre Square and was driving to Claregalway, eight miles away. It was highly uncharacteristic of her not to appear for the changeover as she was a very reliable member of the cabbie's team. A number of phone calls were made to her family in a bid to establish her whereabouts. When it emerged that she had picked up a fare but had not arrived back, her colleagues became very worried. The fact that there was still no response from her radio indicated something was wrong. After a number of attempts to locate Eileen proved fruitless, the gardaí were alerted.

A short time later, her silver 97G Toyota Carina was found abandoned in the yard of an industrial estate just outside the city. A quick examination of the vehicle's blood-soaked interior was enough to confirm what had happened: O'Shaughnessy had been brutally assaulted. The investigation then switched to finding either a seriously injured woman or, unthinkably, her battered corpse.

Now Eileen's family had to endure the agonising wait. How could they know that the body of their beloved wasn't resting in some cold and rural unmarked grave? Would they ever see her again? Questions like these and other 'what ifs', raced frantically through their minds. And why? Eileen was a deeply religious woman, devoted to her children and a law-abiding citizen. It was beyond belief that she could have an enemy with a reason to attack her in this way.

There was the unbearable thought that she was lying seriously injured somewhere and the more time that passed the less chance she had of survival. The minutes passed like hours, the hours like days.

Almost immediately a full-scale search was launched. Although at this stage the incident had the status of a missing person's inquiry, experienced investigators knew that it was more than likely a murder inquiry.

Unfortunately the winter darkness made it virtually impossible to operate, and so the hunt was scheduled to resume at first light. Even a Garda spotter plane was organised for the mission. Word about the disappearance had somehow managed to spread quickly through the city the night before for, early on that frosty Monday morning, a huge crowd gathered to lend their support. The enthusiastic volunteers were quickly split into parties, and each individual set off that morning armed with nothing more than a determination to prevent the name Eileen Costello O'Shaughnessy from slipping into the missing person's file.

Even though the assumption of the general public was that O'Shaughnessy – if ever found – was now probably dead, the optimistic volunteers were having none of it, believing they would locate her alive.

However, their confidence was to be short lived, for later that morning, the Claregalway farmer reported his finding. The distraught family were brought in to identify the body.

Gardai were baffled; there was no obvious motive. Nothing from Eileen's background suggested her killer was someone she knew and the money from the night's takings still sat in its pouch. The postmortem carried out by the State Pathologist, Dr John Harbison, confirmed Eileen had neither been raped nor sexually assaulted. His findings confirmed that Eileen had died from the severe bruising she received to the head. It was a horrendous slaughter, and there was not a scintilla of evidence to help gardaí establish the assailant's motivation.

Even if the money had been missing, such a level of violence would be unusual in a robbery, especially when carried out in the public vehicle driven by the victim. The sheer savagery of the attack fit the frenzied nature of the disorganised killer. This particularly gruesome random killing was carried out with such brutality that the killer would fit the profile of a psychopath with a history of violence and possibly murder. The motivation would be simply that – murder.

This is one of the most difficult types of murder to solve because there is no link between the victim and the killer. Such a murder is carried out by a risk-taker whose compulsion to kill is paramount. The murderer fit the category of a disorganised killer who did not care about leaving evidence at the scene of the crime.

In this case the risk was increased by driving the taxi back towards the city and abandoning it. The only logical explanation for this action was that he had to get back near to where he lived. An organised killer would have worked that out in advance, whereas this was an example of a highly risky improvisation with the possibility of being caught on video security cameras. Unfortunately the spot where the car was abandoned was not covered.

When Eileen's brother, Martin Costello, went to identify the body he immediately noticed a distinctively large hollow located just behind his sister's ear. He explained,

> Her killer had beaten her so viciously I could
> have fitted my entire fist into the hole he had
> left at the side of her head. That dent was
> actually the first thing I noticed when I saw her.
> It was horrific.

An examination of the car easily proved it had not been taken for a joyride. When it was initially discovered parked outside Lydon's Bakery in the industrial estate, it was found that the contact radio inside the vehicle had been wrenched out with apparent force, ensuring that Eileen could not call for help.

The windows, strangely, were rolled down.

Late night workers remembered seeing a lone male driver exit the car and then run in the direction of a yard situated behind a nearby restaurant. However, other people came forward to say they had seen the man run across the road and jump a wall where he then disappeared into the darkness.

Gardaí, despite intensive investigation, had few leads to follow. The investigation, led by Superintendent Tony Finnerty, involved over one hundred members of the Garda Síochána as well as countless forensic staff. Imagine such well-trained manpower, fully equipped with the necessary skills, and not so much as a weapon was ever discovered.

An exceptionally detailed forensic examination was carried out on the place where the body was dumped as well as on Eileen's car and clothing, and it is firmly believed that advances in DNA science may yet solve this heinous murder.

Trace evidence such as clothing fibres left by the killer is of little value if there is nothing to match it with and it can be assumed that the killer, to avoid detection, would have burnt clothing that would have had extensive bloodstaining.

Notices promising rewards for any vital piece of information regarding the murder were posted on ESB poles and in newspapers. Even the taxi company Eileen had worked for generously offered an enticing sum of money in a bid to lure forward even just one potential witness. But there was no one. At the time, Eileen's grief-stricken brother Martin decided to speak out on behalf of the family. He described their sorrow and pain over their loss and pleaded for anyone with information to come forward.

Like every other member of the public, he openly wondered if we would ever truly know why his much adored sister was targeted that night. He then smiled as he began to speak about Eileen Costello O'Shaughnessy the person, rather than Eileen Costello O'Shaughnessy the murdered taxi driver.

He provided a warm insight into her character explaining how she was an incredibly pious person and would attend Mass every day without fail, even sometimes skipping her dinner break if she thought she could make it to Mass a second time.

Friends and colleagues too were plunged into a mixture of heartache and rage; they just couldn't fathom why.

'When it came to Eileen,' they said, 'anyone who met her, loved her.'

In the immediate aftermath of the murder every lead and half-lead was followed up but like any investigation many led to a blind alley. In July 1998 two detectives from the team travelled to Liverpool to question a man who was reported by two female students to have harrassed them near Galway's Ceannt bus and railway station on the night of the murder.

The man, with drug and alcohol addictions and a psychiatric condition, had been treated in St Brighid's mental hospital in Ballinasloe. He had a conviction for manslaughter in England and was in Galway in November but could not remember details of his movements.

One of the students said that he had been harassing her but

stopped when her friend arrived. As they boarded a bus from Limerick they saw the taxi driven by Eileen Costello O'Shaughnessy pull into the station. However the incident did not lead to any charges being brought against the man.

The O'Shaughnessy murder case remains open to this very day and it would seem to the public that a lot of its content has neither changed nor developed. However, according to Galway Chief Superintendent Tom Monaghan, 'The investigation is ongoing and under constant review. We know a great deal today, and are highly optimistic the case will be solved.' In his summation, Chief Supt Monaghan concluded,

> Indeed, Eileen Costello met a very violent death; many of the gardaí who attended the scene were quite shocked by what they saw, and the fact that she was the wife of a member made it even more poignant. But we never close the book on an investigation and, like I said, we are very confident the culprit will be brought to justice.

Eileen's family believe otherwise. When asked how he felt seven years on, Martin Costello paused thoughtfully before gently replying, 'We know no more today than the day it happened.'

Gardaí have admitted to harbouring suspicions regarding an imprisoned double murderer who is currently serving a sentence in Portlaoise Prison that is unlikely to end during his lifetime. In January 2001 a witness made a statement to the investigation team identifying this man, Thomas Murray, as being close to the crime scene as it was being sealed off.

Thomas Murray is a forty-year-old Galway native. Described by gardaí as a 'vicious monster', Murray created havoc in the July of 1981 when, at seventeen years of age, he murdered his elderly neighbour, seventy-one-year-old farmer, William Mannion, a crime for which he subsequently received a life sentence. At the time of his arrest a shameless young Murray even boasted to gardaí that he had planned Mannion's murder well in advance. This statement is likely to be a lie.

Medical files from 1981 revealed Murray suffered from depression and had serious psychological problems. Frighteningly, almost a decade on, in the May of 1990, a prison governor noted that Murray still appeared to have 'genuine psychiatric problems'.

Eileen O'Shaughnessy's murder in 1997 is one in which many people, including gardaí, are convinced Murray is the man responsible. He lived just fifteen minutes walk away from where the taxi was found. However, after intensive Garda interrogation, not once did Murray even so much as slightly falter.

Martin Costello and his family know of Thomas Murray and remain undecided as to whether or not he is guilty.

> Eileen was very tough and streetwise; she would have put up a good fight. So how do we know there weren't two attackers with her in the car that night? But on the other hand, he [Murray]

has no firm alibi for that Sunday evening and, when you think about it, no murder like Eileen's has happened since he was locked up. Without good, dependable DNA evidence, we don't know what way to look at it.

Sadly, he holds little hope of his sister's murder case ever being solved, and readily admits this is one chapter in his life that will never be completely closed.

When gardaí released just brief reports of Eileen's vile and bloody death, it sent shivering shock waves rippling down the spine of every taxi driver, both male and female, working on the road at the time. O'Shaughnessy's brutal slaying highlighted the underlying perils associated with the job of taxi driving. Perils, it seems, that are only too often ignored. A woman died, and what has been done to ensure the same situation doesn't happen again?

A plaque, sitting at the entrance to the boreen on which Eileen was murdered, pay's beautiful respect to her precious memory, but what has our government done for the safety of the drivers in the seven years gone by? Was that murder case not their cue to stand up and make everyone pay heed to exactly what Eileen went through that fateful night? To maybe begin revolutionising the way in which taxi drivers are made to operate? To maybe understand that many taxi drivers now feel compelled to carry some form of weaponry underneath their seat, because they know a panic button won't actually save them? To maybe ensure that Eileen's colleagues all over the country are protected from the likes of the inhuman savage she carried in the back seat of her silver Toyota Carina on the night of November 30, 1997?

In the years since the murder 10,000 people have been interviewed and 3,000 statements taken by the investigation team. The murder of Eileen Costello O'Shaughnessey remains unsolved and her family's grief unresolved.

6

THE MURDER
OF NANCY NOLAN

Bean Uí Nualláin - A Woman of Substance

This loving mother
Nurtured her own
Fostered their talents
Each one of six
Treasure child, now adult
She gave them wisdom.

A presence of substance
Mortal body, life snatched – gone
But immortal spirit never goes
Just like her own 'host of golden daffodils'
Fresh, faithful and uplifting,
She now transcends an awful darkness.

At your little front gate
The serene silence
Enveloping the pastoral view
Of simple sheep on Lisquell
Is fractured by rising traffic
We'll pause – and pray

In all our admiring hearts
You live on.

> Extract of a poem
> written in memory
> of Nancy Nolan

Thomas Murray grew up in Cloonlyon, Ballygar, a small rural village in the north of County Galway. Described by many as a 'slow learner', Murray was apparently a 'very quiet young boy' until he reached his teenage years. This period of Murray's life saw his character transform significantly from a shy boy to a vicious young thug. His family constantly faced accusations that their son harassed and intimidated locals.

In 1981, at seventeen years of age, Murray developed a strong dislike for a female neighbour. He sent her a number of obscene letters and was the eventual suspect in an attempt to burn her car. In that same year the teenage Murray brutally murdered Willie Mannion. The elderly bachelor died after having been stabbed seventeen times in the head and body.

Two weeks after the murder Murray was questioned by gardaí. The next day Murray was found slumped across his bed, unconscious after taking an overdose of pills prescribed for his mentally handicapped brother. Two months later he admitted to the motiveless murder in a statement.

In September of that year he was remanded to St Patrick's Institution and in November a report containing an apt description of his character was compiled. The report stated that Murray was 'emotionally immature with a surprisingly low level of intelligence' and stated that he was a 'borderline psychotic with some element of schizophrenia'. As a result, a medical officer recommended his transfer to the Central Mental Hospital in Dundrum.

The murder trial took place on February 22, 1982, while Murray was still in the Central Mental Hospital. During the trial, Murray gave no evidence, preferring instead to simply plead guilty. He was sentenced to life imprisonment. It appears that Murray remained in the Central Mental Hospital until April 13, 1983, and the only hint on his medical file as to his condition is the word 'depression'. This is a common condition among psychopaths, and the consequent low self-esteem can prompt violence and murder to achieve a sense of status.

It was in 1987 that Murray requested to be transferred to an open prison. However his application was rejected due to the seriousness of the crime for which he was convicted. Then in 1990 the Sentence Review Group examined his file. The group read psychiatric assessments as well as reports from the gardaí and the prison governor. In a report dated May 1990, the deputy governor of Mountjoy Prison stated that in earlier years, Murray 'appeared on several disciplinary reports, mostly for failing to obey orders and that, while one could not possibly tolerate that kind of behaviour, he gave the impression that he had genuine psychiatric problems at that stage.'

It was in November 1991 and on the recommendation of
the Sentence Review Group that Murray was transferred to
the training unit of Mountjoy Prison. Later that year,
however, the group stated that in order to rehabilitate
Murray, he should be transferred to the medium security
Castlerea Prison. They then suggested that subsequent
'occasional temporary releases' be considered, and should
begin with supervised visits to shops. Concerned gardaí stated
that Murray was still very much a feared figure in his native
Ballygar, and suggested strongly that temporary release be
refused.

The warnings from gardaí were completely ignored and
Murray was released occasionally on supervised visits home.
Not long afterwards, he began work in a community work
scheme in Ballinasloe. In 1994 Murray was on one week
temporary release followed by one week in prison. This
arrangement later progressed to ten days temporary release
followed by four days in prison. By March 1995 he was on
fortnightly renewable temporary release, but his release was
not renewed in September 1996 after local gardaí reported
that he had broken his midnight curfew, had made lewd
suggestions to young girls and was suspected of setting fire to
materials and hay belonging to a local guard.

Gardaí once again emphasised the threat Murray posed,
and warned that he was capable of a second murder. There
was still a very real fear of him in Ballygar, they said. As a
result, Murray was returned to Mountjoy, but was transferred
to Castlerea the following December to allow temporary

release for Christmas. His release programme was interrupted on several occasions in 1995 and 1996, including after the murder in May 1994 of Galway woman Philomena Gillane, when 'local people began to fear his presence in the area'.

In the April of 1997 Murray began work as a builder's labourer in Galway. A report from probation officials the following September concluded that Murray's release programme was going well. However, on July 31, 1998, the luxury of temporary release was revoked after he was convicted of indecent exposure in Galway city. This resulted, on September 7, 1998, in six months incarceration. Astonishingly, the following January he was once again approved for accompanied outings, this time to visit his mother who was reportedly dying.

The indecent exposure gave further clue that Murrray was a dangerous psychopath with a twisted attitude to sex and women. He was a loner who had, it has been said, a sick penchant for animal torture. One person recalled how a teenage Murray once took pleasure in shooting dead a donkey, another sign of a psychopath in the making. In fact, while he was incarcerated in the Central Mental Hospital, there were four other inmates who had killed animals as a prelude to becoming murderers.

Anyone with a cursory knowledge of the reports of the Behavioural Science Unit in Quantico, Virginia in the US, which pioneered studies of psychopaths and serial killers, would instantly recognise that Murray is a killer for whom a life sentence should mean exactly that. Unfortunately that was not the case in this instance.

In 1998 Murray, who had been working at the time at a building site near Merlin Park about a mile from Galway City, was taken in for questioning in connection with the 1997 murder of Galway taxi driver Eileen Costello O'Shaughnessy. However, after a full twelve hours of intensive Garda interrogation, Murray still insisted on the authenticity of his alibi. This was the very 'alibi' that consisted of nothing more than a few statements made by the occupants in his lodgings in Ballybane, not far from where the taxi was found. They each maintained that he was present in the house on the night of O'Shaughnessy's death. However, none of the tenants saw Murray in the house that night, they just heard the radio on in his room. This was adjudged enough to have him freed from Garda custody.

At first, many people around Galway did not believe that Murray was the man responsible for O'Shaughnessy's murder, for the simple reason that Murray apparently could not drive. It later emerged that in the months prior to O'Shaughnessy's death, Murray had been taking driving lessons while on release. Although gardaí believe that Murray is O'Shaughnessy's assailant, they have insufficient evidence to prove their instincts are right.

Psychological assessments conducted in 1999 frighteningly revealed that Murray 'had a kink in his personality in relation to women'. However, probation officials maintained that, in order to give him some kind of incentive to re-establish himself, he should be considered for unaccompanied release.

A probation officer within the prison noted that:

> Thomas Murray's thinking is highly distorted in
> his personal relationships and a vindictive and
> petty side of his personality frequently seen in
> prison, is tied directly to his offending.

The same probation officer also recommended that an in-depth enquiry into the views of the Ballygar residents be conducted before Murray was allowed further release.

At a further meeting in 1999, serious concerns were raised regarding Murray's scheduled overnight temporary release. However, the meeting concluded with the agreement that if Murray's father collected him from the prison then he would be released for one day every two weeks. This was to be the programme of releases put in place as part of a process to reintegrate him into society. The situation was reconsidered and as a result Murray was allowed out each Monday. It was on one of these Monday's that his murdering hand struck once more.

On Valentine's Day, February 14, 2000, Murray broke into Nancy Nolan's house and waited for her to return from the supermarket. Nancy, just shy of her eighty-first birthday, had lived alone in her two-storey house since the death of her husband, Thomas, in 1995. As she entered her house – which was just two miles outside Ballygar on the Galway Roscommon border – with her shopping bags, Murray emerged from his dark hiding place, and with a lump hammer, viciously clubbed to death the one person that had risked befriending him while he was out on release.

One of Nancy's daughters who lives in Dublin became concerned when she was unable to make contact by telephone and asked a neighbour to check up on her mother. It was in the early hours of February 15 that Nancy's battered, lifeless body was found lying in a pool of blood on the floor just inside the front door of her house.

In the days after the murder, one of the most intense investigations ever seen in the West was launched and a massive hunt began.

On the evening of February 25, gardaí issued a statement appealing to members of the Ballygar community for any information. While emphasising that the success of the Garda investigation depended on the full cooperation of all, a spokesperson stated that the community 'owe it to the memory of the much loved and respected Nancy Nolan, and to themselves, to ensure that the perpetrator of this heinous and brutal crime is brought to justice.'

Nancy, who lived across the road from the primary school in which she had taught with her late husband for forty years before she retired in 1984, was a highly respected figure within the Ballygar community. She was known to be 'very active', well-liked, and was described on several occasions as being a 'loving mother' and 'a devoted grandmother'.

Gardaí believe Murray bore a grudge against Nancy Nolan – a former primary school teacher of his – and had harassed her in the past. However, in a typically Christian act, she had refused to shun him and was seen talking to Murray a week prior to her death. Just five months before the murder, a meeting at Castlerea Prison heard that Murray was 'greatly feared' in the locality and that any overnight stay there would 'cause a panic'. Gardaí classified him as being 'dangerous and unstable', and Garda sources have since admitted to being 'absolutely furious' that he was granted temporary release from jail in the first place.

Meanwhile, Nancy Nolan's funeral mass in Toghergar church saw one the largest crowds ever to attend the church. The removal of the remains which were scheduled to leave the funeral home at 8.30, did not leave until ten o'clock due to the large numbers that came to pay their respects.

A team of forty gardaí, led by Roscommon Chief Superintendent Bill Fennell, was involved in the investigation. Inside sources admitted to being 'baffled' by the absence of an apparent motive for Nancy's murder. The team would discover that a psychopath requires no other motive than the act of killing.

On February 21 gardaí stopped motorists at checkpoints around Ballygar for five hours in an attempt to jog the memories of anyone who might have seen anything unusual in the area the week before.

Hundreds of families spoke to gardaí making door-to-door enquiries, while 1,200 questionnaires were distributed to homes and business premises over a large area in another bid to jog memories. In early March RTÉ's *Crimeline* programme broadcasted security film footage of Nancy shopping in

Ballygar on the morning of February 14. An appeal was then made by Chief Superintendent Fennell to anyone with 'even a scrap of information'. Although there was a good response to the programme, nothing of significance turned up.

Around this time, Justice Minister John O'Donoghue found himself under immense pressure to elucidate exactly how the temporary release programme for convicted killers is controlled.

Fine Gael's Jim Higgins, put his position on the matter on record:

> It has been well known that there have been serious problems with the temporary release scheme. Many prisoners are released without any supervision whatsoever and there does not appear to be any real mechanism where gardaí can air their concerns about individuals. I will be demanding to know who made the release order and why the objections of the gardaí were not adequately considered.

The murders of Nancy Nolan and Eileen Costello O'Shaughnessy bore strikingly similar traits in that neither woman had been sexually assaulted but had each received very severe bruising to the head and face from a heavy blunt instrument. Gardaí also noted that in both murder cases nothing was stolen from the scene of the crime, which immediately implied that the killings were not driven by an obvious motive such as robbery or rape.

Two months after the Nolan murder, thirty-six-year-old Thomas Murray (who was still serving out his sentence at Castlerea Prison) and his sixty-eight-year-old widowed father were arrested and questioned at Roscommon Garda station in connection with the killing. Both men were released without charge. Thomas Murray was later again arrested and questioned. He was held under Section 4 of the Criminal Justice Act and, on this occasion, gardaí had his period of detention extended somewhat. Murray was released from Garda custody without charge.

However at 10.25 a.m. on June 1, 2000, he was arrested once more and cautioned by Detective Sergeant Tom Fitzmaurice at Treanrevagh, Mountbellew in Galway. It is said that Murray, who initially denied involvement in the murder claiming he was elsewhere at the time, changed his statement and admitted to the killing. Half an hour later he appeared before Mountbellew court and was charged with the murder of Nancy Nolan. During the Mountbellew hearing, Detective Sergeant Tom Fitzmaurice told the court that Murray made no reply when told of the charge. While his defence solicitor Gareth Sheehan applied for full legal aid, Murray, dressed casually in a white open-neck shirt, green jumper, blue jeans and white runners, sat silently in the third row with his head bowed.

During the court appearance, Sheehan told Judge Michael Connellan that he believed Murray was in need of full-time psychiatric care at that time. Judge Connellan said that, although he would note this, he was not in a position to make any order in this regard.

That morning, groups of onlookers gathered in the rain outside Mountbellew court until Murray eventually emerged from the building, surrounded by Garda detectives. He was then taken back to Castlerea jail in a Garda minibus. The following week on June 7 Murray appeared before Ballinasloe District court.

On December 5, 2000, thirty-seven-year-old Thomas Murray was given a life sentence in the Central Criminal Court after he pleaded guilty to the murder of Nancy Nolan. The court was told that Murray carried out the murder while on day release from Castlerea Prison where he was serving life imprisonment for the murder of seventy-three-year-old Galway farmer Willie Mannion in 1981. Justice Paul Carney was told how the victim was 'a kindly woman who showed no animosity towards anyone' and that 'there was absolutely no reason and no motive whatsoever' for the murder. Those attending the court listened in silent shock as they were told how the eighty-year-old woman died from severe head trauma.

Although Murray initially denied the killing, forensic samples of polyester fibres taken from the deceased matched those found on the accused's clothes. In a number of signed statements Murray made to gardaí, he pinpointed the exact location of the deceased's spectacles and the murder weapon. Both items were found as a result of his statements. His defence counsel, Patrick Gageby S.C., told the court that Murray wished to apologise to the family of the deceased and to express his deep remorse. It is a known fact that such killers experience neither inhibition about carrying out the crime nor remorse. Therefore it can be taken that Murray's statement was to in some deluded way mitigate responsibility for his heinous act.

Nancy Nolan's son, Hugh, and her five daughters, Ann, Noreen, Sheila, Louise and Eileen sat in the court and witnessed the mandatory life sentence being handed down. They said that they were still trying to make sense of their mother's murder. After the conviction, a member of the Nolan family criticised the unsupervised temporary release that Murray was enjoying when he bludgeoned Nancy to death. Her six children also demanded an investigation into how Murray could have carried out the brutal crime and then return to prison the same day without the prison authorities noticing anything.

As Hugh Nolan said:

> Questions must be asked about this whole issue,
> about how our mother's killer was allowed out
> on day release. This man was a convicted killer.

Gardaí expressed satisfaction at the outcome of the trial and credited its success to the good groundwork of gardaí combined with that of the forensic and technical experts. However, although Murray was convicted, the controversy surrounding the case was far from over. Many were now accusing the prison system of 'lax handling' of a man convicted not only of murder, but also the second offence of

Bernadette Connolly

Kerrie, Ann and Patricia Connolly at Bernadette's grave. (Brian Farrell)

Cloonmahon Monastery, the focus of Bernadette Connolly's murder investigation. (Brian Farrell)

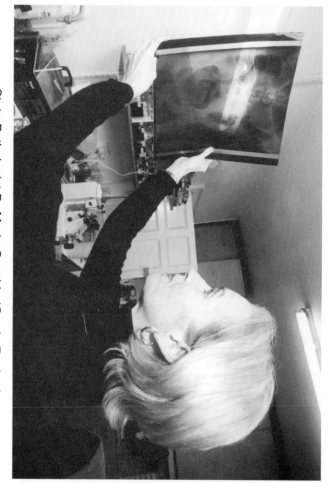

State Pathologist Dr Marie Cassidy (Garda Review)

Dr Marie Cassidy approaches a crime scene with members of the Garda Technical Bureau. (Collins Photo Agency)

Memorial at the location of Eileen Costello
O'Shaughnessy's brutal murder. (Tara King)

The laneway in Claregalway where Eileen
O'Shaughnessy's body was found. (Tara King)

The popular taxi driver
Eileen Costello O'Shaughnessy. (Tara King)

Nancy Nolan

Thomas Murray (Collins Photo Agency)

Kevin Reilly

Kevin Reilly's
father, Joseph

Brian Murphy's parents (Collins Photo Agency)

Brian Murphy's family outside the court. (Collins Photo Agency)

Nichola Sweeney

Peter Whelan (Collins Photo Agency)

Catherine Kealy

Lorraine O'Connor, a radiant teenager.

Noel Hogan (Collins Photo Agency)

The building where Lorraine O'Connor was murdered. (John Galvin)

indecent exposure, a crime he committed while out on temporary release. As a result, Murray saw his routine change to a day-release programme whereby he was released at 9 a.m. and was required to return to prison by 8 p.m. every night.

This was the very release programme he was on when he murdered Nancy Nolan.

Following the outcry regarding temporary release of convicted murderers, a report on the management of Murray's sentences was undertaken by former senior civil servant John Olden for the Department of Justice. On July 6, 2001, an official report into the murder of Nancy Nolan was released. But rather than quell the growing controversy surrounding unsupervised prisoner releases, the report created further arguments. Although it recommended that procedures be tightened, it firmly maintained that inmates should still get such freedom, as constant confinement would severely hamper the rehabilitation process.

Castlerea prison governor Daniel Scannel noted that Murray had nineteen unaccompanied temporary releases in the months prior to the murder. However the Department of Justice revealed they had no record of Murray ever being granted unaccompanied release in the first place. In the report the Justice Department said it had not agreed to changing Murray's temporary release programme from accompanied outings to unaccompanied releases in September 1999, however Castlerea Prison insisted that the relevant permission had been given.

The report said this disagreement was 'to say the least, disturbing'. The Department of Justice report into the case found that there was 'a difference in the appreciation of what had been decided (or not decided) in relation to outings for Murray as between the local prison records and the Departmental (prison headquarters) records.'

Mayo Fine Gael TD, Jim Higgins, immediately sought a full Dáil debate on the report.

> The minister [John O'Donoghue] must explain the blatant contradictions between the prison service report and what was on file in the Department of Justice. He must also explain why the fears of the gardaí, strenuously put on more than one occasion, were apparently ignored.

John Olden's report also honed in on a comment made by Governor Scannel which was recorded in the minutes of a review meeting that took place on October 27, 1998. Governor Scannel had warned that Murray would 'kill again if ever released'. Upon learning of this 'pre-warning', the public demanded to know why that same governor introduced a temporary release programme for Murray in 1999. The then Prison Service Director General Sean Aylward stated that Scannel's comment was made in light of arguing for further therapy for the killer. According to Aylward,

> The governor had sought his release for good

reason because the original offence had taken place nineteen years earlier and, while there had been concerns in recent years about him, Thomas Murray had been through seventy-three sessions of counselling and the governor felt it was a reasonable risk to let him out.

Scannel also agreed that the comment had to be taken in context and that, after a lengthy process of engagement with the probation and welfare officer, his concerns regarding Murray were reduced significantly since he made the warning. He had chaired subsequent meetings in which a temporary release programme for Thomas Murray was discussed, and Scannel says he gave 'verbal assurance that he was not in opposition to such a programme'.

The report recommended that

> Prisoners like Murray should immediately receive therapy on imprisonment and not after seven years in custody. Prisoners like Murray who commit a significant breach on temporary release should have their cases fully reviewed before any further releases. The Justice Department and Prison Service should adopt modern procedures for assessing the prospective danger posed by releasing prisoners.

The report revealed the various objections lodged by gardaí in relation to Murray's temporary release. Gardaí had objected on the grounds that it would 'constitute a threat to the community'. They also said that Murray was a person of an 'extremely violent nature' and unless he had totally transformed himself, he continued to pose a very real threat. But John Olden maintained that 'gardaí were generally opposed to, and critical of, decisions to release people who had committed very serious crimes.'

A major overhaul in the way in which 'lifers' are managed was ordered after the independent report highlighted the various weaknesses in the system. It called for the tightening of procedures and a general review of the temporary release of inmates who committed violent crimes.

The report also suggested that there should be no 'skimping' on the number of staff assigned to deal with the administration of sentence for 'lifers', and that all formal tools be used to evaluate a prisoner's 'prospective dangerousness'. Justice Minister John O'Donoghue requested that the then Prison Services Director General Sean Aylward implement all the recommendations made in the report as well as taking whatever other steps were necessary.

Aylward stated that

> Even with perfect hindsight, Murray's risk factor would not have indicated that he might suddenly murder while on a one-day release.

In July of 2001 the family of Nancy Nolan apparently discussed taking civil action against the prison authorities, for they believed that this would be one way of highlighting the prison release of Thomas Murray. Nancy Nolan's sister Eileen Glynn, from Ahascragh in County Galway, criticised the way in which the report into the controversy was released by the Department of Justice on Friday evening, July 6. She said,

> They release it on the Friday evening to the media, the day on which the Dáil breaks up for the summer. The family are not told about it. It looks like they are trying to put their own slant on it.

Eileen, originally from Castlerea, said she established through her own contacts that the report had been with the department 'for a while back'.

Nancy Nolan's brother, Colm O'Callaghan said that he was not happy with the Olden report as there was a lot of 'passing of the buck from one to another'. He also stated that the report had not answered any questions for the family adding that, if anything, the report and the media publicity surrounding it's publication had caused them distress.

In his report Olden found that

> Murray got a good deal of attention from the relevant services, in particular from the Probation and Welfare Service, members of which, in the period between August 4, 1998, and February 24, 2000, had seventy-three meetings with Murray including eight meetings each in the months of November 1998 and January 1999.

Olden also goes on to say that

> It is quite clear from reading the papers and talking to the persons who had dealt with him professionally that, like many other persons who have committed murder, Murray had a difficult personality and would need a lot of attention before he could be safely released back into the community.

On the other hand, the psychiatrists and the chief psychologist who interviewed him during the period of his sentence considered him not mentally ill.

> Having spoken to various persons who were familiar with Murray's behaviour while in prison, I conclude that he would be generally regarded as being socially inadequate but that on the other hand none of the staff, including the female staff, were afraid of him. In fact, he had never got into any serious trouble in the whole nineteen years of his imprisonment. Significantly he appears never to have engaged in violent behaviour while in custody.

On the subject of prisoners out on unsupervised release, Olden concluded,

> I think it would be a reversal of policy and a real mistake to take the easy way out and say that no risk will be taken in future. That essentially

would be a political decision but one with serious consequences. The vast majority of persons sentenced to life imprisonment do not seriously re-offend after release.

Prisoners without any hope of early release pose special problems and if the numbers of these prisoners increased because of over-cautious policies, very serious incidents within the prisons would become much more likely. Unfortunately, there will always be some prisoners for whom that prospect, punctuated perhaps by periods in the Central Mental Hospital, is unavoidable.

Nancy Nolan's daughter Eileen, who was two years ahead of Murray in primary school, is still searching for answers. In January 2002 she said,

The answers we have got have raised even more questions. We know it will never bring our mother back but the least we are entitled to is to know what happened. What we want to know is what rehabilitation programme was put in place for Murray? How can a governor of a prison say 'if he is released he will kill again' and then sanction his release? Obviously a mistake was made, a fatal error . . . There has been a serious system failure somewhere.

While no one individual in the chain can be held responsible for what happened, the result of collective deliberation was catastrophic. Previous experience in the US and the UK has shown that psychopaths are highly skilled at fooling seasoned professionals about the state of their mind.

In Britain there is recent evidence to demonstrate that three psychopaths fooled the professionals in the parole area who judged that not only were they rehabilitated but also capable of being safely released. All three went on to kill again. One murdered three times after being released. What the Irish authorities need to learn is that there are killers who are beyond the so-called norm of what the system wants in terms of rehabilitation.

Long before that system messed up in the case of Thomas Murray, it took on board the horrendous crimes of John Shaw and Geoffrey Evans for the murders of Elizabeth Plunkett and Mary Duffy in 1976 and Malcolm McArthur for the murders of Bridie Gargan and Dominic Dunne in 1982. Those killers will rightly remain in prison.

There are many others who are in prison with the possibility of release and who will then kill again. Until legislation is introduced to make sentencing fit the crime, the current flawed matter of discretion will lead to further killings. The victims of heinous murder and their relatives deserve better than the wind of political whim to establish the fate of the architects of their unending misery.

I will leave the following Dáil exchange between Jim Higgins TD and Justice Minister O'Donoghue, expressing the parlous state of the lack of specific legislation, to ring in the ears of the dead and the living victims.

Dail debate
Subject: Nancy Nolan / Thomas Murray
February 21, 2002

Mr O'Donoghue:

. . . it is true incidentally that in nearly all cases, the gardaí caution against releasing individuals. As I have said, one cannot operate a system of release, where one is trying to reintegrate individuals into society, without their being some risk, however small.

Mr Higgins:

To say this was a 'system failure' is a gross understatement. Will the minister apologise to the Nolan family for the manner in which the State neglected to protect their loved one? Does he accept that the warnings of the Garda Síochána in this case should have been heeded? The individual concerned was a murderer with a series of breaches of the terms of his early release. Will the minister have the matter investigated again given that the Olden report contains a mass of contradictions in relation to the different versions of events which should have been unravelled and resolved? The head of the person responsible for authorising this individual's release should roll.

Mr O'Donoghue:

I am deeply sorry that this should have occurred and I have extended my sympathy to the family. I am deeply sorry on behalf of the Department, the Prison Service, the then Government, and this Government. The situation is, unfortunately, that an offender, for example, who is up for release may have committed even the crime of murder perhaps several years ago or when he or she was very young. It does not mean one can then reasonably conclude that for the rest of his or her life that propensity to kill or cause injury would be such that conditional release could never be contemplated.

We could not operate a system like that in any kind of humanitarian regime. It is true that, looking back on what happened here, it is a grave tragedy that the individual was ever released. Of that there is no doubt. I confess it is not an exact science. Had I been minister when the original temporary release was granted, I cannot, hand on heart, say that I would have said 'no'.

7

KILLING OUTSIDE CLUB ANABEL

It was a sultry night in August, the last day of the month, and a night made for young people to enjoy themselves. Young men and women with no real responsibilities, their holidays over and glittering careers stretching before them. They gather in clubs and pubs, exuding life and energy, high fashion, style and the evanescent beauty of youth. On this night around 700 young people had converged on Club Anabel in the Burlington Hotel on the south side of Dublin where there was a drinks promotion.

They came from predominantly middle- and upper middle-class families and many of the young men were in college, having graduated from the exclusive school stables of Blackrock College, Clongowes, St Mary's College and Terenure College, schools with strong histories and associations with the Leinster Schools Rugby Competition.

For the majority it would be a long night's journey of enjoyment but for a very small group the early hours would lead to the very heart of darkness.

The previous day a number of Blackrock College graduates had got together before the late night outing to Anabel's.

Andrew Frame and Dermot Laide went swimming in Killiney with Alan Dalton and Shane Fallon. Frame and Laide had maintained close contact since their time as boarders in the Southside school where they had both been prominent players on a winning senior cup rugby side.

Andrew Frame had just finished the first year of an economics course at UCD, while Dermot Laide, a student at the Dublin Business School, had been accepted on a sports management course at UCD. Their other friends, Sean Mackey and Desmond Ryan had been day pupils at the same time and were also bound for UCD, the former to pursue an economics degree and the latter to study agricultural science.

That evening Frame and Laide, with Alan Dalton and Shane Fallon, dropped into the Magic Carpet off-licence in Cornelscourt, South County Dublin to purchase cans of Bulmers cider and bottles of Smirnoff Ice.

Dermot Laide from Castleblaney in County Monaghan was staying with Alan Dalton and had not come prepared for socialising. He went to a shopping centre to buy a toothbrush and razor blades. They went back to the Dalton household where they were joined by a larger group of young men including Seán Mackey.

Brian Murphy an eighteen-year-old who had attended Gonzaga and Bruce College was also planning to go to Anabel's that night and he decided to wear a distinctive maroon Lacoste polo shirt. Brian was a keen soccer player but naturally he had come across boys from other schools, including Blackrock College. While at Bruce College he befriended Barry Cassidy who knew the Laide and Frame group when he was a pupil at 'Rock.

Michael Hussey, a Clongowes boy, knew Brian Murphy for several years and had recently become close friends.

Alan Leonard who would arrive at the club later that night with the Frame-Laide group had been in the scouts and played soccer for Mount Merrion Football Club with Brian Murphy. Elizabeth O'Mahoney, Seán Mackey's girlfriend, was a neighbour of the Murphy family and the sister of Brian's best friend. There were several other connections between all these young men. It didn't matter what school they attended, it was a small world.

In the summer of 2000 Brian Murphy had a job working in the storeroom of Brown Thomas with his close friend Matthew Moran. Brian had never been to Club Anabel but a barman told him that he could get on the guestlist which meant no problems at the door. The friends met up later at the Sports bar in Belfield on UCD campus and took a bus to Appian Way where Moran needed to get his ID card from a younger brother before going to the Burlington a short walk away.

As they went into Club Anabel Brian Murphy pointed out a number of young men from Terenure. A few weeks earlier he had had a disagreement with some ex-Terenure College boys over somebody doing something to his ex-girlfriend. There had been another confrontation outside a bar two weeks earlier. Such confrontations, fights and disagreements are commonplace among young men of that age and, though there are exceptions, these result in little more than bruised egos.

When a friend, Louise Geraghty, met him inside the club, Brian Murphy told her that he expected to be beaten up by some boys from Terenure College. She told him to go home. His friend Matthew Moran was buying the drink because Brian did not have much money, and those who met him said he was merry as opposed to drunk. There were many others who were having more than their fair share; despite the lower cost of drink at promotions, young people tend to tank up in advance of going to a club.

David Cox, a former Blackrock boy, had drunk five half-litre cans of Heineken before leaving for the club, a naggin of vodka on the way, and then four pints and two bottles of Smirnoff Ice in the club. Former Clongowes boy Fiachra O'Brien had six cans before going out, a pint in a local pub, then five or six bottles of Smirnoff Ice at the club plus some shots. Another Clongownian, Morgan Crean, had three pints of Carlsberg in a local pub, and another three pints of Heineken and three shots in the club.

Matthew Moran had between five and ten pints and he reckoned Brian Murphy had a similar amount.

Andrew Frame had six pints of Bulmers before going out, followed by two long-neck bottles of Bulmers and a vodka and blackcurrant at the club. His friend Dermot Laide had drunk two cans of Bulmers and four bottles of Smirnoff Ice in the house but when he arrived at Anabel's he was refused entry and had to hang around outside for a number of hours waiting for his friends to come out. Seán Mackey, according to people in his company, had a considerable amount to drink.

As the night came to an end Matthew Moran, Brian Murphy and a group left the club, some of them rolling joints and smoking outside. Close by, Aisling Walsh left with a group of friends. One who was quite drunk sat down on a kerb and took her shoes off. One of the youths took her shoes and would not give them back. It seemed like a bit of light-hearted banter but when one of the youths threatened them, it took a nasty turn and the girls got upset.

From decades of experience of club-goers spilling on to the streets in the early hours, recorded incidents show that it can be an extremely dangerous time. But this was not a venue where such danger was a common occurrence. There was an incident in which Brian Murphy was peripherally involved where a milk carton was stolen from a float and thrown. Michael Hussey was there and admitted throwing the carton. The milkman gave chase and a group began to sing 'hail to the driver'. Hardly something that could be interpreted as anything but laddish behaviour.

The crowd of 700 was spilling onto the relatively small area at the side and front of the Burlington. There was bound to be some jostling. According to Michael Hussey Brian Murphy bumped into someone and there was a verbal exchange. Out at the front gate some slagging carried on between a group including Hussey, Brian Murphy and Andrew Frame. Frame was the object of the slagging and told the group to 'fuck off'.

This seemingly meaningless encounter led to a fight, the

details of which are to this day unclear and cannot be established with any degree of certainty other than the consequence: Brian Murphy threw a few punches, was hit twice by Dermot Laide, and then viciously attacked by others and kicked to death.

Brian's friends took his prone and now unconscious body across the road and rang for an ambulance which took him to St Vincent's hospital. He died a short time later.

Subsequently Dermot Laide, Desmond Ryan, Andrew Frame and Seán Mackey were charged with the manslaughter of Brian Murphy. Two and a half years later, on January 13, 2004, the trial began in the Dublin Circuit Criminal Court before Mr Justice Michael White and a jury and was to last six weeks.

The Verdict Feb 25, 2004

Having been earlier warned by Mr Justice White about reporting restrictions on the case, the media had to be circumspect about dealing with the verdicts and the general reporting was suitably sober.

The following morning *The Irish Times* report ran:

> One of the four men who has been on trial in Dublin for the last six weeks in connection with the killing of student Brian Murphy outside the Burlington Hotel in August 2000 was convicted of manslaughter. A second man was acquitted of violent disorder.
>
> This morning, after spending a second night in

a hotel, the jury of eight men and four women will resume its deliberations on the two other accused.

Dermot Laide (22) from Castleblayney, Co Monaghan, was found guilty of manslaughter by a 10-2 majority. He was also found guilty, by unanimous decision, of violent disorder.

Mr Andrew Frame (22) from Nutley Lane, Donnybrook, was acquitted of violent disorder.

Earlier in the trial he was found not guilty of manslaughter by direction of Judge Michael White, who said there was insufficient evidence against him.

Mr Desmond Ryan (23), from Cunningham Road, Dalkey, and Mr Seán Mackey (23), of South Park, Foxrock, are still awaiting verdicts on the charges of manslaughter and violent disorder against them.

Judge White remanded Laide on continuing bail to await the outcome of the jury's deliberations on Mr Ryan and Mr Mackey. He told Mr Frame he was free to go.

The four accused had denied charges of unlawfully killing eighteen-year-old Mr Murphy after a fight outside the Burlington Hotel on August 31, 2000. The four former Blackrock College students had also pleaded not guilty to using, or threatening to use, unlawful violence.

> Mr Murphy died from swelling to the brain caused by severe facial injuries after he had been attacked by a group of up to six youths following a student night out in Club Anabel in the Burlington Hotel.

Feb 27, 2004

Desmond Ryan was acquitted of the manslaughter of Brian Murphy. The jury failed to agree on a manslaughter charge against Seán Mackey.

Both had already been convicted at Dublin Circuit Criminal Court of violent disorder outside Club Anabel.

Judge White remanded Laide, Mackey and Ryan on continuing bail until March 8. He told the court that after that he may need approximately a week to consider the sentence. He listed the outstanding manslaughter charge against Mackey for mention on the same date. Mackey was subsequently found not guilty of the charge.

Judge White discharged the jury from the trial and excused them from further duty for life. He said to them:

> I have to pay a heartfelt tribute to you for your dedication in this trial over the past seven weeks. Your public service as jurors has been exceptional and you have spent great time deliberating on this jury.

Laide was sentenced to four years for the manslaughter and a concurrent two years for violent disorder. Mackey was sentenced to two years, and Ryan nine months for the violent disorder convictions. All three have lodged appeals.

The conclusion was an anticlimax and this last dark day reduced many present to tears. Despite the rigorous pursuit of the law, the punctilious conduct and utter fairness of the trial judge and the dedication of the jury, there was no sense that the wheels of justice had turned as they should have done. The final curtain was greeted with silence.

Three women and two men of the jury cried openly, the forewoman rubbed her reddened eyes and another man buried his head in his hands. Dermot Laide's girlfriend broke down in tears and was comforted by a friend. Brian Murphy's parents cried inside, though they did not show it, but his sisters did as the jury filed out for the last time. For the relatives and friends of the victim those tears will never cease.

The grief of the relatives of the victims of violent crime and in particular of the murdered or killed is further intensified by the trial process. This is mainly due to the adversarial system of law in which the counsel for the defence and prosecution engage in a protracted argument often over many days and, as in the Anabel case, at times in the absence of the jury. Often at the centre of argument are the Rules of Evidence which for many observers are complex.

The victim's father, Denis Murphy, in his address to the court summed up everything that is wrong with a system that is pitched firmly in favour of the perpetrators of crime.

> As a result of the past seven or eight weeks there are now more questions than answers. There is

only evidence of one kick being delivered
despite the general evidence that there was a
wave of feet and that people were behaving like
animals.

I also found that the trial process was not about
finding the truth but about shamelessly avoiding
it, if it were not on your side. Before this trial the
family were doing well but now there is a gaping
wound. I'm not sure where we will go from here.

It is a horrendous indictment of a system that a trial that lasts
so long and costs such a huge amount of money cannot
establish what exactly happened on the night and who was
responsible for the death of Brian Murphy. It was accepted by
the court that Dermot Laide was only one of a number of
youths who attacked the victim and his involvement was not
solely responsible for the horrific injuries sustained by the
victim. He threw two punches; others kicked the victim while
he was down on the ground.

Many times the trial ground to a halt and the jury shuffled
out of the court so that a legal argument could help the judge
determine what was or was not admissible in evidence.
According to Ludovic Kennedy, a well-known campaigner
against the miscarriage of justice, in a system whose object is
to find the truth, 'there is very little evidence – so long as it is
deemed relevant – that is not admissible'.

The Murphy family might not be surprised to learn that
some of the most eminent figures in the law from all parts of

the world – including that great champion of justice Ludovic Kennedy – entirely agree with Denis Murphy's assessment of our justice system.

The adversarial system was a relatively late development in English law and then evolved, in the words of Charles Langbein, Professor of Law at Chicago University, 'slowly, incrementally without plan or theory, until it became the top-heavy, artificial creature it is today'. Until well into the eighteenth century, criminal cases were heard without counsel and the trial judge was both examiner and cross examiner as he or she is still in France today.

William Hawkins, writing in *Pleas of the Crown* in 1721, argued that this is how it should be:

> The very speech, gesture and countenance of those who are guilty, when they speak for themselves, may often help to disclose the truth which would probably not be so well discovered from the artificial defence of those speaking for them.

This system, where the accused is compelled to be examined, is the inquisitorial system, practised in Europe today.

In France in the eighteenth century the examining magistrate or *juge d'instruction* chose the prosecution witnesses. In England there was no such process, so bounty hunters and accomplices turned King's evidence. It was to prevent such self-servers from helping to convict – at a time when petty crimes were hanging offences – that defence counsel began to emerge.

Having successfully challenged the evidence of Crown witnesses the defence found that there was no need to call evidence from the accused. It was these steps that led to the accused being given a right to silence. Later, the accused under the Criminal Evidence Act could not be convicted on the word of an accomplice. It is a system in which the accused is perceived to be the most important person in court, the belief being that the defendant has the most to lose. Which is rather contradictory. The victim has lost his or her life and the family and relatives have been consigned to a life of loss and suffering. The accused faces a loss of freedom which, in the main, means anything but a life sentence.

The adversarial system is open to abuse, as when the prosecution fails to supply evidence to which the defence is entitled. The trial process allows a spurious sense of drama to be created which encourages counsel to take postures and attitudes and indulge in insults and sarcasm. The counsel see it as one of their tasks to destroy the credibility of the other side's witnesses on issues which may or may not be relevant to the case.

In many cases the neutral observer could be forgiven for assuming that the witnesses were also on trial and not present to determine the truth.

Questions that could provide a shortcut to the truth are not allowed and others which are asked are not allowed to be answered. Evidence of witnesses is shaped by what the prosecution and defence want them to say or what they think the prosecution or defence thinks they should say. Other witnesses whose evidence might help to shape the jury's verdict are not called for fear they will say the 'wrong' thing.

It is a system in which evidence given or suppressed can lead to the innocent being found guilty, and the skills of counsel in many cases have set free the guilty.

As Ludovic Kennedy remarks:

> Is this really the best we can do? If we were devising a new system of justice today from scratch, would it ever occur to us to dream up something either so complicated or so inefficient?

Some of the top international legal minds have given their views on the system that so upset the family of victim Brian Murphy.

Justice Geoffrey Davies, Queensland Court of Appeal: 'The adversarial system operates unfairly in that, both in specific cases and by its general operation, it causes injustice to those who are affected by it.'

Nicholas Cowdrey QC, New South Wales Director of Public Prosecutions: 'The adversarial system is not directed towards the ascertainment of truth, despite our pretences to the contrary . . . In our system a lawyer with a client works hard to avoid justice being done, or even worse, the truth being discovered.'

Judge Harold Rothwax, New York: 'Our system is a maze of elaborate and impenetrable barriers to truth . . .

Suppressing evidence is suppressing truth . . . Without truth there can be no justice.'

Sir Laurence Street, former New South Wales Chief Justice: 'Truth and justice require a moderation of the extreme adversarial system and the abolition of the rules for concealing evidence'.

John Dobies, distinguished Sydney lawyer: 'Once we are in court we play this game called Courtroom. The idea is to win this game.'

Geoffrey Robinson British QC and author of *The Justice Game*: 'Is it a game? Yes. Should it be? No.'

Professor William Pizzi, former US prosecutor: 'Even those who work the system, don't respect it.'

Denis Burke. Chief Minister and Attorney General of Australia's Northern Territory: 'Our justice system, per se, is totally, totally corrupt.'

From some of the most eminent and respected practitioners of this system this is damning and concurs with the experience of the Murphy family and other families of victims dealt with in this book. If the trial process can prove farcical it is equalled by sentencing policy. This is not only widely divergent but also fails to take into account the fact that certain forms of killing indicate quite clearly to investigators and forensic psychiatrists that the perpetrators will when released be almost certain to repeat the sort of crime for which they have been convicted.

While these crimes may be at the top of the scale, some of the sentences in so-called 'killing without intent' also do not reflect the seriousness of the crimes committed and the devastating effects on the families of the victims. In the killing of Brian Murphy, it was not just a matter of a simple punch thrown with accidental consequence. That does happen but many cases involve a concerted effort in which the line between intent and accident is infinitesimal. If a knife or a gun or a constant and sustained kicking to the head is the cause of death are we to suppose that the perpetrators had no idea of the consequence of their actions?

How long does it take to have an intent to kill? The young men who are responsible for the death of Brian Murphy may not have set out that fateful night at Anabel's to kill but, once involved, by delivering a flurry of kicks to the head of a young man, who had already been struck and was on the ground, must have intended great damage and known that this action could result in the death of the victim.

It was argued by the late Greg Murphy S.C. while defending Mark Nash, who was accused of the double murder of Carl and Catherine Doyle, that his client had never set out on the night in August 1997 with the intent to kill. He had not the necessary intent, *mens rea* in law, to qualify for murder – he should be tried for manslaughter. The sequence of events was as follows.

On the night in question Nash had travelled with his girlfriend Sarah Jane Doyle to the home of her sister Catherine and her husband Carl in Roscommon. After being collected from the Dublin train they went back to the house where they drank alcohol and smoked cannabis. Later on in the evening Nash felt sick and went to the toilet where he suffered a bout of vomiting and diarrhoea.

At some stage one of those present took a photograph of Nash on the toilet. He reacted to this with a sudden rage, and a compulsion to kill overtook him. He first attacked his girlfriend with an iron implement and then took a boning knife from the kitchen and savagely attacked Catherine and Carl, killing them both. Sarah Jane survived and Nash was arrested in Galway the following day.

While Greg Murphy's defence that Nash may have been guilty of manslaughter but not murder was rejected by the court there was some merit and a certain logic behind it. Nash and his girlfriend were having problems and the trip to Roscommon was to get a break in the country with her sister and husband in their rural idyll. Nash had absolutely no motive to kill anyone and, in the early part of the evening, no intent. The alcohol and drugs consumed were of relatively modest proportions and at any rate Nash's sickness would have flushed much out of his system.

So he is sitting on the toilet, his trousers around his ankles, and there is a flash of a camera, perhaps a laugh. Suddenly he becomes a killer and tells Sarah Jane, 'You have to die.' Later Nash said he could not explain what came over him, it just happened. This is an entirely different scenario to someone getting a gun or any other weapon and deliberately going out to kill, but once the thought entered Nash's mind the intent kicked in.

For the family of Brian Murphy the inability of the system

and trial process to establish and punish those responsible is galling enough. But further insult is heaped upon them by the cursory sentences handed down to those who, their defence teams would say, were peripherally involved. The fact that they have appealed those sentences is rubbing salt in the open wounds of the Murphy family.

There is also the suspicion that someone out there knows who delivered the fatal kicks to Brian Murphy's head while he was on the ground.

A Mother's Plea

It is undoubtedly true that even those journalists who have spent most of their career covering trials for murder and manslaughter, or writing about crime have but a scant grasp of the misery that such events visit on the families and relatives of the victims. The grief of affected families can only be understood on the surface; only their testaments can give an insight into the devastating effects they suffer as a result of the taking of their loved ones' lives.

On Monday March 8, 2004, at around 11.30 a.m. Mary Murphy addressed the Circuit Criminal Court and gave a moving, articulate and heart-rending account of the impact of the death of her son Brian on her and her family. No interview could have replicated this epic expression of the tragedy visited on the Murphy family.

She first leant across to Judge Michael White to present him with her favourite picture of her dead son along with a memorial card. Then for thirty minutes she addressed the court in a quiet determined voice.

I am here for Brian. This is the most nerve-wracking thing I have ever done. I'm doing it also for myself because I have been forced to keep silent for so long. But my real motivation in taking the stand here today comes from my deep love for my son.

The love that one has for one's child is primal. It's the type of love where you would put your own safety at risk. It is the only comparison I have for the love that God has for us.

I was not there when Brian was savagely kicked and beaten to death. If I had been there you would not have succeeded in your quest to attack my baby because you would have had to kill me first.

I spent a lot of my time over the past week preparing a text for this impact statement. It contained details and a description of how I felt in the immediate aftermath of Brian's death, how we were told not to touch his body in case we would destroy evidence. There were details I wanted to share about Brian's wake, his funeral and his burial. When I read it over in preparation for today, it sounded so hollow. When I asked myself why did I feel this way, the feeling came that apart from the judge and my own close family and friends the rest of those listening to me probably did not want to know. When I thought about that I realised how much I have felt under attack in this courtroom over the past seven weeks.

I will try and outline why I felt this way.

Firstly, when I woke up the next morning still thinking about this, I noticed as I lay in bed that I had my two arms tightly over my face and there was huge tension in my whole body.

In a strange way I felt that there was an uncanny resemblance between Brian's predicament in his final moments and my feelings of being surrounded by people whom I felt didn't want to know about our tragedy.

Just thinking about our family's seating in Court 23 helps me to further enhance what I'm talking about.

In front of us were seated the prosecution barristers and solicitor. Beside them were the defence barristers and their solicitors. The media and the accused were also present. All of these people had a voice. Brian and our family, I felt, had no voice. That is why I felt surrounded and under attack.

I would like to describe how I felt about these various parties.

First of all we heard the prosecution, who don't represent Brian, but who act on behalf of the people of Ireland and therefore represent the State. I felt the rules governing how they were allowed to argue the case to be so restrictive. To me the evidence of some witnesses was confusing and contradictory, yet the prosecution was not able to recall these witnesses for clarification.

Then we have the defence teams. The main effect that the defence had on me was that I felt that I was being brainwashed into thinking that what happened to Brian was somehow his own fault. The repetition of evidence over and over again somehow desensitises everyone to the reality of what happened to Brian.

The summing up of the defence tried to paint all the defendants in such a wonderful light, that it was a tragedy for them to have to be sitting here as defendants at all. Are you allowed, in summing up, to blatantly contradict a scientific witness such as Dr Harbison, who stated that Brian consumed less than twice the legal limit of alcohol permitted when driving a car? This means that Brian consumed between three and four pints on the night in question. In the summing up there was a suggestion that he consumed twice that amount.

Then there is the media. I think the message abroad from the media is that the tragedy of our own family and those of the accused is, in some way, comparable. The opinion of the general public seems to suggest that any of their children could have been involved in a similar attack. It was a tragedy for these guys. The headline in one Sunday broadsheet epitomises what I'm saying, where Brian is described as 'The Luckless Murphy'. This suggests that poor Brian was just unfortunate to be in the wrong place at the wrong time.

The biggest fault that I have become aware of as I have read some media is that they are quoting as fact something that has been alleged, and are using that to back up their own agenda. This has the cumulative effect for me of diminishing Brian as a human being. I would just like to clarify that I have felt that direct evidence quoted by the reporters which speak directly about the evidence as presented before the jury has been, in my opinion, for the most part accurate. But remember, this is only evidence. People who swear before God to tell the truth, the whole truth and nothing but the truth, don't necessarily do that.

And, finally you have those convicted of their part in Brian's killing, who have attempted to deny and minimise their part in Brian's death.

So, maybe now you can understand why I

could not share my innermost feelings about my beautiful darling son to a listenership such as this.

So I don't intend to go into any great detail about how it felt to watch Brian as he lay dead on a hospital bed with his two front teeth smashed; or about the long wait before his body was brought back home in a coffin to us; what it was like to watch my child lie in a coffin with my rosary beads wrapped around his hands and Brona's private letter to him lying on top of his body.

I have an abiding memory of so many candles lighting all day and all night in the room with him. I am not going to tell you about the prayers of forgiveness, which we composed ourselves, and which we brought before God at Brian's funeral Mass. I won't attempt to describe the devastation I felt at Mount Jerome crematorium, as the curtain went across Brian's coffin to the music of Brian's favourite song, 'November Rain', or about the box of ashes I carried to his grave.

I was going to describe the emptiness in my heart and in my home, about the weeks and months afterwards when I prayed that I would die too, about the anger I felt towards God because I felt that He could have stopped this.

The delay in the trial process added hugely to
our pain.

So where is my baby in all of this? I can't find
him. He's lost. I'm lost. All my family and friends
are lost too.

Where is my pride and joy, my full of
confidence child, my crazy, exuberant, full of
cheer, larger than life child. My naïve, far from
perfect child who did some silly things and some
fabulous things.

On the basis that the judge does want to know
who Brian was I will attempt to introduce you to
this dehumanised by the trial process Brian
Murphy. Actions speak louder than words.
Anyone who saw the video of Brian interacting
with his little brother on TV should be able to
see the vitality, the warmth that was in him as he
rubbed the top of Robert's head after he kissed
him and used the words, 'I love you too, Baby.'

Here is my humble attempt to describe
Brian. Anyone who knew him would say that he
was a free spirit who was larger than life. He had
a special charm that drew people to him. He was
eighteen, remember. He had still a lot of
maturing to do both physically, emotionally and
mentally. He was highly intelligent. His
exuberant personality refused to be quashed.

As a person, Brian had time for everyone. He

labelled no one. He had so many friends from all schools and our local soccer club. His friends came from every walk of life and every background. He was not an adopted Clongownian. He liked people for who they were and nothing else. What schools people attended was irrelevant to him.

He was a brilliant listener. He made you feel you were important to him. He was so open. There was no pretence. What you saw and heard was the real him, warts and all. He was an individual with his own views. He was a leader. His sense of humour was second to none. To remember him is to smile He would introduce humour into the everyday, the banal. The spirit that was Brian was manifested in his appreciation of the finer things of life.

At his funeral Mass a young lady told a story about Brian from the altar. How he brought her into the National Gallery to show her, in his own words, the best painting ever. It was a painting called The Opening of the Sixth Seal, the theme which was taken from the Book of Revelations in the Bible. It was painted with a black background with a red sun, and orange and red flashes of lightning. He was fascinated by it.

He loved poetry. I vividly remember the days prior to his Leaving Cert English exam of him showing off how he could recite every poem on the course, even though this wasn't necessary for the exam.

He loved mountains. His favourite holiday was one we spent camping in the Alps. We have put a picture of Mount Fuji on his memorial book mark because that is a place he longed to visit. In a book where he had read about Mount Fuji, called *The Natural Wonders of the World*, Mount Fuji is described as a place of pilgrimage and a sacred place, the reason being that its coned peak goes above the clouds, and there is an air of heaven and earth coming together at its peak.

Dr Harbison said that Brian had a slightly enlarged heart. Clare said to me afterwards that was a good description of Brian; that is, that he had such a big heart. Stories of Brian's big heart abound. The one that sticks in my mind happened the summer before Brian's death.

He came with me and Robert to visit my mother, who was suffering from Alzheimer's disease. She was in a nursing home in Bray. We walked to the seafront with her, with Brian holding her hand. Brian gave her a cigarette, and we laughed as she tapped the ash in the way she would have prior to her illness.

Brian put his arm around her and said, 'Gran,

I'm sorry I haven't been to see you in a while,' and he started to cry. She did not understand a word he was saying. He then went to the seashore with Robert to show him how to skim stones on water.

He was delighted at Robert's success in doing this and gave me the thumbs up from the water's edge. Robert remembers this day also.

There is a story of him bringing home, unbeknownst to me, a man who was down on his luck to our home and him cooking one of his specialities for him.

To me he was my best mate. I had completed first year as a mature student in UCD in the faculty of social science. I found studying for the exams really tough. Brian was there for me with his encouragement to keep at it. To his delight I passed my exams. During that summer I worked as a social care worker with a young girl who was a heroin addict.

I found the work emotionally draining and Brian was a ready listener when I descibed to him what life was like for this young girl.

What I miss most of all about Brian is the fun we had together. My best memory of this is our day together on his eighteenth birthday. We went into town and bought his present, having travelled to every shop in town. I will never forget the camaraderie there was between us as we chatted over lunch in a restaurant chosen by him.

He told one of his friends, speaking of me, 'Mary understands me.' I am so glad that he said this as it gives me huge consolation.

How do I convey how Brian's death has affected me? The pain I felt was physical. I could not shed a single tear, which would have been an outlet for some of the pain. The pain was one of shock, numbness and grief which had no outlet because I could not cry. In time with the feeling of anger came the tears which at least gave some release to the pain.

I have and will continue to have great difficulty letting myself feel the sadness. Devastation is more the word to describe it. I have to blank that out. This will never go away and it is something I have to try to accept.

Then I think of what it was like for Brian in his final moments. What was the horror and terror like for him? He must have been pleading in his mind, 'Will somebody help me?'

This talk about Brian's group. What group? If Brian was with a group he would still be alive because they would have come to his defence. The boasting and cheering are scary, like we have gone back to the dark ages. Words like manslaughter and violent disorder make killing sound respectable. This I find nauseating.

I wonder what legal jargon would be used if Brian hadn't died but was left brain-damaged, with the suffering that would have been for him and us. Denis and I have lost our beautiful son's future – his maturing, his becoming more sensible as he got older. But the biggest thing we have lost out on is his sense of fun.

Robert was six years old when his brother, whom he loved, was snatched from him. Robert started playing matches for his football club a year after Brian died. Brian would have been his number one supporter on the sideline, offering all sorts of advice to his little brother. Denis said just after Robert was born that he was looking forward to the day when Brian, Robert and himself would attend matches together. This never happened. I imagine the slagging there would have been between them over premiership results, Brian being a Spurs supporter and Robert a Liverpool supporter.

All Robert has left of Brian is his picture which he has pasted to his bedside locker, a teddy Brian gave him, and an old Spurs shirt of Brian's which Robert sleeps on when he is feeling particularly sad. Robert goes through phases of sadness. It usually happens at night when he cries and says, 'I miss Brian.' I hate this loss for Robert more than anything.

Brona told me of an evening when he arrived home when she was babysitting Robert and he walked in and said to her 'Brona, you know I love you.' This coming from an eighteen-year-old boy to his fourteen-year-old sister shows what a special person he was. There are sixteen months between Clare and Brian. They were like peas in a pod, doing everything together.

What effect has the trial had on me? I'm back to when Brian died. That we should be forced to revisit it after three and a half years is inhuman. The shock, the anger, the sadness are back and along with these is fear which must be present as a result of hearing the details of what happened to Brian. I wonder will I ever feel safe again, because the way the justice system works makes me think we live in a a very unsafe society.

I wanted questions answered by coming to this trial every day. The way I see it, there was no fight when Brian was killed. There was a concerted savage attack where he was surrounded and kicked to death.

I feel brutalised by this trial process. The quest for the truth becomes a battle between two sides caught in a game, each side trying to win points. Brian gets lost. Brian becomes the object in the red shirt. There are some phrases that are ingrained in my mind and will be with me for the rest of my life:

'We got him good.'

Other witnesses used another version of this which I prefer not to repeat.

'This is great craic.'

'Behaving like animals.' As a lover of animals I find that remark insulting to animals.

'He fell flat on his face with no arms to save him.'

'I started all this.'

'The wave of feet.'

'I couldn't put faces to feet,' by witnesses who knew the accused.

The new shoes kicking him. The big-headed guy who walked away from the group kicking Brian.

'I heard his head snap, crack and I felt it go soft.'

I used to think that whoever did this will have to live with it for the rest of their lives, which is why I prayed for them and their families at Brian's funeral and at subsequent anniversary Masses.

After attending this trial and hearing what I have heard, I don't think that anymore. They just want to get off.

If they had a conscience and if they were really sorry for what they have done, they would tell the whole truth about what has happened, own up and take the consequences.

Truth is lost here. Brian is lost here. I am lost here. I have agonised over forgiveness over these past years since Brian's death, how I couldn't find it in my heart to forgive. I wasn't going to pretend to forgive, it had to come from my heart.

From the way this whole case has gone, I am clear on one thing. I cannot contemplate forgiveness until I know the truth and those responsible for Brian's death have acknowledged their part in it and make known the part others played in his killing.

The anger I felt mounting as the trial progressed was all about what I have just said, that nobody was owning up. The way I see it, that is the only way of getting on with the rest of your lives. There is no way of hiding from the truth. It demands to be seen and heard.

On considering this issue for myself, I was reminded of the account in the Bible of the crucifixion of Jesus, where the two criminals were on crosses on each side of him. One said to Jesus, 'If you are king, you save us.' The one on the other side said, 'Leave him alone, he has done no wrong. We deserve to be here, he doesn't.' Jesus said to this criminal, 'You will be with me today in paradise.' He did not say it to the other one. The man who told the truth won the favour of Jesus.

To conclude, we as a family have to go from here to try and get on with our lives. I know that in time and with God's help, as I move through all the pain that is ahead of me, that I will survive as Brian has survived. I know for Brian that life has changed, not ended. I am not afraid of death any more. I look forward to running into Brian's outstretched arms, as he enfolds me in his warm, joyful embrace.

I have a memory which convinces me of Brian's state. Some months after his death I was coming out of a deep sleep when I heard his voice in my head, which just said, 'Sorry'.

He had come back to say this word to me. It was a word I was used to when he was alive. Whenever we had words, which mothers of teenagers often do, he would be heading out afterwards and he'd shout, 'I'll see you, Mum.' Then he'd have qualms of conscience about what had been said and he'd arrive back and say 'Sorry, Mum' about whatever the disagreement had been about. I'd say, 'It's okay, Brian' and he'd head off much happier. The fact that Brian came back and said this word to me is a sign to me that he is still alive.

I am so thankful for the support I get from my husband Denis and my three other children. I hope I can support them also. I am so thankful for the support of the rest of my extended family and for the support of our good, honest, trustworthy, faithful and loving friends.

Can I make an appeal to the media? Please don't misquote me, or quote me out of context. Please, please respect my integrity. It is so hurtful to see yourself misquoted or the wrong slant put on what you say. If you care in any way about me or Brian and my family please take the time to understand what I'm saying. I feel the lives of those convicted in connection with Brian's death are not ruined, as some media have said about them. They are not ruined if they can summon up the huge courage that is needed to face the truth.

The truth will set you free.

The sentiments and emotions expressed by a mother grieving for the tragic loss of a son crucified by kicks instead of nails are searing with honesty in an arena awash with dishonesty where the truth got as bad a battering as Brian Murphy. Such was the emotive power of Mary Murphy's speech that families and friends of everyone involved in the court sat numbed in an overcrowded and airless room. Some wept silently or shifted uneasily during the passage where Mary described what it was like to see her dead son lying in a hospital bed, unable to kiss or hug his humiliated, crumpled human remains for fear of disturbing evidence.

The images that haunted her were equally graphic and haunting for those looking on. One could only wonder what effect they had on those involved in the killing. Brian lying in the coffin with his mother's rosary beads threaded through his fingers, the candles burning night and day, the private letter from his sister lying on his body.

In the brutal flurry of kicks and punches in 'getting him good' could they have imagined what devastation and grief they were heaping on an innocent boy and his family who had never done any harm to anyone? Had they even a whiff of the endless misery they were going to cause, every ordinary experience of a family relationship now couched in painful significance.

Mary Murphy painted a picture of a loving young man and her words resonated with the truth. He was also an eighteen-year-old boy who possessed the faults of any teenage male growing up in an increasingly predatory world.

Mary Murphy's words were still echoing around the courtroom when the legal process, but not her life, moved on. The defending barristers rose to makes pleas of mitigation for the accused. Those involved in this heinous act, he said, had done good deeds in their time and now their lives were set on hold, plagued by stress-related illnesses and the knowledge that they could not walk down the street again without being recognised as one of the 'malefactors in this case'.

The last part is disingenuous to say the least. It might have been the case during the trial, but now nine out of ten people would not recognise the accused on a crowded Grafton Street. The families were hard-working decent people. Father Aidan Troy the Belfast priest said of the Laides:

> To say that this was a very wealthy posh family
> rearing a family of brats is so far from the truth
> that it breaks my heart. I know a lot of people
> who are richer than the Laides.

None of this, like much of the argument in the trial, had anything to do with the central fact: a young man was savagely beaten and kicked to death. It mattered not a whit what sort of background the perpetrators came from. Rich kids or poor kids, a death is a death. Does it mean anything to the Murphy family whether the people who kicked the life out of their son had a degree or a prison record? They came seeking the truth and justice and they got anything but this basic right.

The defence lawyer Anthony Sammon S.C., doing his job like all the rest, said that 'the spark of conflagration was lit by Brian Murphy'. If the rest of the conflicting evidence and contradictory eyewitness accounts are to be taken into account that fact may be questionable. But even if we accept this as the truth, does a boy who is responsible for a spark deserve to be burnt to death?

Mary Murphy's justifiable response to this, another

insulting legal red herring, was to mouth a silent protest and leave the courtroom with her daughter. It was a sad anticlimax after her powerful evocation of the tragic effects on her and her family of that fateful August night.

8

JUSTICE DENIED – THE KILLING OF KEVIN REILLY

It was a scenario that we have read about in the newspapers dozens and dozens of times. A group of youths meet in a green area of a working-class estate. Words of banter then aggression are exchanged. Suddenly one pulls out a knife and lunges at another. The rest of the youths scatter. The stricken youth falls to the ground, his life blood pumping from a gaping wound.

An ambulance is called and a Garda patrol car arrives on the scene. When the ambulance arrives, the paramedics work feverishly to resuscitate the youth. The ambulance rushes to the nearest hospital where the youth is admitted to the casualty department. The staff on duty spring into action in a quiet and efficient way.

By then the relatives of the young man have been informed and arrive at the hospital, not understanding what has happened and in a state of shock. In the dull corridor of the general hospital, with the impossibly overworked casualty department just a door away, they await the news with trepidation.

The minutes feel like hours. A nurse comes. Things are not looking good. How has this happened? Why? The nurse comes back with a garda. The young man has been pronounced dead. The garda asks a member of the family to come to another room to identify the body.

The father goes with the garda into a room off the casualty area. In a bed he sees his son. He looks as though he is asleep. The garda tells him of the incident on the green earlier. The medical staff did everything they could. Too late. The doctor pronounced him dead ten minutes ago.

The blood has frozen in the father's veins. His youngest son wouldn't hurt a fly. A loving boy, a great little footballer. Was never in trouble with the law. We had our arguments, that's natural. We had one the night before. So what? Dead? Can't be. I should be dead first.

A numbness came over his body and enveloped every part. He heard his words, in the distance telling the garda that yes, this was his son and giving the address of his home.

A nightmare had begun, a nightmare that would never end.

This is a typical story. A true story with subsequent twists that intensified the tragedy.

The nightmare for Joe Reilly and his family began on April 15, 1992, when his son Kevin was stabbed to death not far from their home in Jobstown in Tallaght. Kevin had been hanging around the Cloonmore estate with his friends Paul Monks and Gavin Daly when they encountered a number of other youths they knew, including Sean McCallan. Gavin

Daly, his brother Daniel and Sean McCallan had been involved the previous evening in a fight in which the brothers had given McCallan a beating.

Kevin Reilly was not involved in that incident and was nowhere near the location where it took place. Daly asked McCallan if he remembered anything about the night before. McCallan said he did. A conversation ensued between the youths who had been involved in the fight. There was a suggestion that someone in the group call over for another youth, Scully, but nobody wanted to because his mother had just come out of hospital. Daly invited McCallan to fight but he declined.

After a verbal exchange, McCallan suddenly pulled out a knife and lunged at Kevin, the innocent bystander, who dropped to the ground. After taking a few steps towards Gavin Daly, McCallan ran off.

Kevin Reilly was not answering to his name. Monks ran to Kevin's mother's house and an ambulance was summoned.

Later on that night Kevin Reilly was pronounced dead at St James's Hospital. He was sixteen years of age, an innocent who lost his life, literally for nothing. McCallan was charged with the murder but after a four day trial in the Central Criminal Court which began on February 15, 1993, he was acquitted on the grounds of self-defence.

Since the trial, as in the Brian Murphy case, left more questions than answers the most accurate record of the events on the evening of April 15, 1992, are contained in the coroner's inquest which took place in the Dublin Coroner's

Court on June 17, 1993. In a criminal court witness statements are defined as evidence, while in the coroner's court they are called depositions and the statements are given by deponents. The deponents are sworn under oath just as witnesses are in the criminal arena. A file is prepared of the depositions in advance of the inquest hearing which is, in the metropolitan area, heard before Dr Brian Farrell, coroner for the City of Dublin, and a jury.

While the coroner's inquest is a legal process just like a trial, it is conducted, from my experience of attending many, not just with thoroughness and professionalism but also in a far more humane fashion. The relatives of the victims are treated with the respect that they deserve. Dr Farrell, as well as being punctilious in his handling of the proceedings and direction to the jury, always has words of kindness and genuine concern for the relatives after the verdict has been announced.

This is not in any way to diminish the trauma of the father, mother, siblings or relatives listening to the last hours or minutes of a loved one's life but in the coroner's court, one can be sure that respect and sympathy are part of the agenda. That, as little as it might seem, means a lot. In the criminal court, as we have discovered, fact is a matter of interpretation and argument. Truth is not at the top of the agenda.

In the coroner's court fact is paramount. Therefore the truth will follow. In the case of the killing of Kevin Reilly the truth emerged not in the criminal trial but in the record of the coroner's court proceedings.

An ambulance assistant attached to Belgard Fire Station, Hugh Madden, told the inquest that while on duty on April 15, 1992, there was a call to the station at approximately 9.25 p.m.

> I accompanied Terry O'Neill to Rathminton Court, Jobstown West, Tallaght. On my arrival there at 9.34 p.m. I observed members of An Garda Síochána having an open space there sealed off. We were directed to this area. I saw the body of a youth lying on the grass verge. We immediately gave the youth medical aid.
>
> He had a wound on the upper left side of his chest. He was not breathing. We then placed this youth on a stretcher and placed him in the rear of the ambulance. I was joined by Garda Mannion in the rear of the ambulance. The body was taken to the casualty section of St James's Hospital. With Garda Mannion I continued to give cardiac resuscitation to this youth but, unfortunately, it had no effect. At St James's Hospital the body of this youth was handed over to the medical staff of the casualty section.
>
> We also conveyed another youth, who was conscious, to St James's Hospital at the same time. This youth had an injury to his left hand. His name was Gavin Daly. We arrived at the hospital at approximately 21.43 hours.

Garda Paul Gaynor of Tallaght Garda Station told the inquest:

> While the injured person was being operated on
> I met a youth who asked me how he was and
> that he had done it. I asked this youth his name,
> address and date of birth. He gave it as Sean
> McCallan, 23, Cloonmore Green, Tallaght,
> Dublin 24. Sean McCallan was then taken for
> treatment for injuries to his hand. Garda
> Mannion stayed with him at all times. At 10.12
> p.m. on April 15, 1992, the injured person was
> pronounced dead by Dr Una Geary. I met a man
> in the casualty department who said that his son
> had been stabbed in Tallaght earlier. The man's
> name was Joseph Reilly.
>
> At this stage I returned to where Sean
> McCallan was sitting and I asked him what had
> happened. He told me the following which I
> made notes of in the presence of Garda
> Mannion.
>
> 'I was going down Rathminton with Tracy
> Fitzgerald. He [Gavin Daly] kept going on at me
> for a fight and Kevin, the red haired fella,
> started pushing me too. He kept slagging. He
> kept pushing. I had a knife. I took it out. I
> stabbed him. I don't know where. I don't know
> what happened after. I stabbed the two of them
> with a kitchen knife. It was all over last night.
> There was a big fight. I stabbed Kevin Reilly and

Daniel or Stephen Daly. I brought the knife home and threw it in the kitchen.'

He signed the notes after I read them back to him. Garda Mannion and myself also signed these notes.

At 10.51 p.m. on April 15, 1992, Joseph Reilly identified the body of the dead youth as Kevin Reilly of 21, Cloonmore Lawns, Tallaght to me.

Paul Monks, Kevin Reilly's friend, lived at 14, Cloonmore Green. On the evening of the stabbing he called round to Kevin's house. They watched television for a while before going out to call on Kevin's girlfriend Jennifer but Jennifer wasn't there.

This is Paul's account of the events that led up to the killing:

Myself and Kevin started to walk back to Cloonmore and Gavin Daly came out of his house and called us. We stopped and Gavin Daly came up to us. The three of us started walking up through Bawnlea. Gavin Daly started telling us about a fight he had the night before with Sean McCallan who lives in Cloonmore Green.

He told us that himself and his brother Daniel were up at Rathminton. Gavin said that Sean McCallan and a fellow called Scully from Sundale started chasing himself and Daniel.

They were throwing rocks at them. Gavin said that himself and his brother ran and when Scully and Sean McCallan ran out of rocks, they ran back towards them. Gavin said that himself and Daniel caught McCallan and gave him a beating. Gavin also said that Sean was drunk. Gavin said that after that they went home.

Kevin, Paul and Gavin then met four other youths in Bawnlea and kicked football with them for a while before walking to Rathminton.

We were walking along the bungalows at Rathminton and we saw a fellow walking towards us. Gavin and Kevin thought this fellow was Kevin Carroll.

When this bloke got closer I noticed it was Sean McCallan from Cloonmore Green. Gavin Daly called Sean over to us and asked him did he remember anything about last night. Sean McCallan said 'Yeah'. Gavin then asked Sean was he hurt and Sean said he couldn't feel anything because he was so wrecked [meaning drunk]. Sean had a cut on his bottom lip and Gavin asked him what happened to it. Sean said 'You did it', meaning Gavin and Daniel Daly. Gavin then said 'Did we?' and Sean said 'Yeah'. Gavin and Sean started getting smart with each other.

Gavin then asked Sean to call up to Scully and ask him to come out and have a straightener [a fight] with him. Sean said no, that he wouldn't call up to him because Scully wouldn't come out. Gavin and Sean started arguing about calling up to Scully. Sean then pointed at me and Kevin and said to Gavin, 'Send one of them in to knock for Scully.' Gavin said to Sean that we don't want to go near Scully's house because his ma was just after coming out of hospital and that he was worried that something would happen to his ma.

Gavin Daly then asked Sean McCallan to fight him on the road. Sean said no, he didn't want to fight anyone. Myself, Kevin and Gavin started laughing at Sean McCallan because he was acting like a coward. Sean had his hands in the pockets of his jacket. When we were laughing at him he just went mad. He took his hands out of his pocket. Sean started shouting and at the same time swung at Gavin with his right hand. I saw that Sean McCallan was holding a knife. I think that knife had a black handle and a blade about four inches long. I jumped back.

I then saw Sean swing at Kevin Reilly. I didn't think that Sean had got Kevin but I saw Kevin falling on the ground. I thought Kevin had tripped up. Gavin started shouting, 'He has a knife.' I ran towards the roundabout. Sean then ran three or four steps towards Gavin. He still had the knife in his hand. Gavin ran away towards Kiltadown. Sean came up to Kevin and looked at him. Kevin was lying on his right-hand side. Sean kicked Kevin in the ribs on his left-hand side and then ran down the road towards the bridge at Cloonmore. I picked up a piece of wood and threw it at Sean, but missed. I shouted 'McCallan you're dead.' Sean started laughing and kept running.

Paul and Gavin walked back to Kevin and saw a bloodstain spreading around the left side of his chest.

Kevin was choking and there were spits hanging out of his mouth. Gavin shouted at me to go down to Kevin's ma and ring an ambulance. I ran down to Kevin's ma's house and told Kevin's brother Christy what happened and he ran up. I knocked on the door and went in and told Mrs Reilly to ring an ambulance.

Joseph Reilly told the inquest of how he found out about the death of his youngest child.

I am Kevin Reilly's father and he lived with me at 21, Cloonmore Lawns. My wife and I have been living apart for about six years. My other children Christy and Bernard lived with my wife at 1, Cloonmore Lawns. My two daughters Lorraine and Sharon are married and have their own homes.

On Tuesday night April 14, 1992, I was at home watching television. At about 10 p.m. Kevin came into the house with Paul Monks from Cloonmore Green. The two of them went up to Kevin's room and were watching television. At about midnight I wanted to go to bed and I went up to the room and told Kevin I wanted to lock up. Paul Monks wanted to stay but I told him to leave. Kevin and myself had an argument about it and eventually I said to him to go around to his mothers. So both of them left and I locked up.

The next day, April 15, 1992, at about dinner time Kevin came in and was ironing his clothes. He said he was going to move back into his mother's as we did not get on. At 7.30 p.m. I went to St Thomas's Church in Jobstown to open up for the 8 p.m. service. At about 9.15 p.m. I arrived home and a neighbour David Brennan told me that he thought that Kevin had been stabbed. I then telephoned the police and the Dublin Fire Brigade and I found out that Kevin had been taken to St James's hospital.

At this point my daughter Sharon arrived and the two of us drove to St James's hospital in my

van. When we arrived I was told that Kevin was
not good by a nurse and we waited in a room.
Some time later, I am not sure of the time, I
went into a room and saw my son Kevin's body.
I went in with a garda and identified my son's
body to the garda.

The State pathologist Dr John Harbison noted in his report to
the inquest:

The principal, lethal non-surgical injury on the
body was a stab wound $1^5/_8$ inches long on the
left side of the front of the chest, 3 inches to the
left of the midline, 2 inches below the left
collarbone and 2 inches in front of the armpit.
There were two stitched horizontal surgical
drain wounds on the left side of the chest, 3
inches and 5 inches below the armpit.

The only other non-surgical injury on the
body was a bruise beneath the nail of the left big
toe.

Dr Harbison's internal examination revealed the following:

The stab wound track beneath the chest wound
passed medially through the first intercostal
space, through the anterior margin of the upper
lobe of the left lung, thence through the thymic
remnant, into the pericardium and thence into
the ascending aorta. The wound in the aorta was

jagged with two notches at its lower end and irregular upper end. The track, finally exiting from the right side of the ascending aorta about 2cm above the valve, grazed the outer layer of the media side of the right atrium of the heart. The wound had given rise to a tamponnade consisting of 190ml of blood in the pericardial sac, mostly clotted. That blood in turn, had leaked into the pleural cavity, which contained 900ml of blood, mostly clotted.

The left lung, as a result was rather collapsed but, on section, dry and healthy looking.

The right lung was profoundly oedematous. It was intact, as was the right pleural cavity. There was considerable bleeding into the anterior mediastinal tissues including the thymus.

The stomach contained fairly recently ingested food which was darkened, suggesting some bleeding into the stomach for which, however, no source was found.

Dr Harbison summarised his findings and concluded thus:

1. The deceased Kevin Reilly, in my opinion died partly of blood loss, that is shock and haemorrhage, but also from an element of tamponnade which means compression of the heart by accumulation of blood in the pericardial sac and around it, preventing

> effective beating. All these findings were due to a stab wound in the ascending aorta resulting from a single stab wound in the front of the chest.
>
> 2. The deceased was healthy at the time of his death.

The inquest verdict stated that Kevin Reilly was pronounced dead at St James's Hospital, Dublin 8 on April 15, 1992, from haemothorax and haemopericardium due to a stab wound to the ascending aorta following a single stab wound to the chest. Death in accordance with the medical evidence.

The inquest provides a very clear picture of the circumstances of Kevin Reilly's death and the medical reasons for the death. This is despite the absence of a deposition from Gavin Daly who was a principal participant in the events of the previous evening and in the verbal altercation that preceded the knife attack on the victim. His deposition would have also explained why he ended up in the ambulance and why Sean McCallan also ended up in St James's Hospital for treatment.

One can fairly speculate, in the absence of his deposition, that there was a further altercation between himself and McCallan which resulted in both needing treatment for wounds that can only have originated from the knife used in the stabbing of Kevin Reilly. Daly's evidence was material to both the criminal trial and the inquest. If Daly gave a statement to the gardaí, and it is inconceivable that an investigation would not include it, why was it not passed on to be included in the coroner's inquiry?

There is little doubt that McCallan felt under threat. He had been beaten up the night before by the Dalys and when he met the three youths at Rathminton, Gavin Daly was present and invited him to fight. Clearly McCallan was not going to trust his fists which had let him down the night before. He had obtained, not what he described to Garda Gaynor as a kitchen knife, but a far more deadly weapon, a butcher's knife used to cut the flesh from animal carcasses. This would cut through a human body with deadly effect.

If McCallan felt threatened then the antidote he employed went far beyond any reasonable strategy for defence. And since Kevin Reilly had not been present during the previous night's altercation with the Dalys, McCallan had no justified fear of him. His problem was with Gavin Daly.

When questioned by Garda Gaynor in St James's Hospital, McCallan admitted that he had attacked Kevin Reilly although his version of events, if we are to accept Paul Monks's account, is not only exaggerated in his favour but he lies when describing Kevin Reilly's involvement in the verbal altercation that led to the stabbing. He claimed that 'Kevin the red-haired fella started pushing me too. He kept slagging. He kept pushing. I had a knife, I took it out. I stabbed him.'

While this is at odds with Paul Monks's account it is a clear admission of responsibility for the killing

Monks describes Gavin Daly as being the main aggressor when they encountered McCallan at Rathminton. There is no mention of pushing and the only thing that Kevin Reilly is doing according to Monks is laughing. He provides no threat, apart from his presence in the group. The main and enduring threat is from Gavin Daly, who, despite all his posturing, has made no physical advance on McCallan.

And yet McCallan pulls out the deadly butcher's knife, makes a lunge at Daly and then swings it at Kevin Reilly, who had not even raised a fist to him, stabbing him in the chest with such force that the aorta was punctured, flooding blood into the chest cavity and lung. Under no circumstances of the facts outlined in the deposition at the inquest could McCallan's action be construed as self-defence in relation to the killing of Kevin Reilly.

In the absence of intent, the action fits the very definition of manslaughter – the unlawful but not deliberately planned killing of one human being by another. Yet McCallan walked free from court by justification of self-defence.

This was an absurd decision. The victim was a young man of exemplary character, footballer of the year in his soccer club and a title-winning GAA player. He had never been in trouble of any kind. The decision of the court in relation to his killing is, just like the Brian Murphy case, another appalling example of the iniquities of the adversarial system which can bend the truth just like Beckham can the ball.

Worse still, it has haunted the family of the victim for the past twelve years, particularly his father Joe who has mounted an unrelenting campaign to highlight the injustice meted out to his son and the family. Joe clearly, physically and mentally, is still affected by the awful events of the evening of April 15, 1992. He is not looking for revenge or a jail sentence, just an explanation of how the system imploded the case. He wants to clear his son's name.

> Kevin was totally innocent, he was no thug, he was never in a fight in his life. When the fellow who killed him said that he did it in self-defence it made Kevin out to be a hooligan and I will do whatever is necessary to clear his name. All I want is the truth and the proof that Kevin was the good child that I know he was. I want his name cleared so he can rest in peace and so I can grieve properly for the loss.

> I have battled for this cause for the past twelve years and it is both emotionally and physically tiring. Kevin's death has consumed me every day over that period of time along with all the unanswered questions about the investigation and of course the sheer injustice of the court decision. Kevin never raised a fist, he is dead. The court accepted a plea of self-defence after a lot of the legal focus was on the fight of the previous evening in which Kevin had no involvement.

> What happened on the night Kevin was killed is straightforward. There were no complications and no doubts and yet what resulted in court was a complete and utter travesty of justice and

a total denial of the truth and real facts of the death of my son who had not an ounce of aggression in his bones and was mercilessly stabbed with a butcher's knife.

Under Irish law self-defence is a complete defence to a murder charge if no more force than was reasonably necessary was used. That was not the case here. When Kevin was stabbed, his heart was punctured; he had no chance of survival. Was this no more force than was reasonably necessary? It was a lot more.

The devastating internal injuries described in the postmortem report back up Joe's view and again make nonsense of the verdict. The clear implication in the verdict that the accused needed to defend himself against Kevin Reilly adds to Joe's grief and continually haunts him. He claims that his teenager son was untruthfully and wrongly portrayed as a thug during the trial. The sixty-eight-year-old former plumber and church caretaker has now secured the support of a petition signed by 18,000 people and many high-profile politicians – including Proinsias De Rossa, Ciarán Cuffe and Patricia McKenna – for the investigation to be re-opened.

So far, apart from the huge groundswell of support which has given him much consolation, he has run into a brick wall with the authorities.

I just want to get to the bottom of Kevin's death

for the peace of mind of the family. I have made every effort to get a copy of the book of evidence but to no avail. I have taken my campaign to the Department of Justice, the Ombudsman, the DPP, The Chief State's Solicitor's Office but nobody can give me any assistance. They all say that the gardaí carried out a proper investigation and they cannot comment on how the trial was conducted.

The mantra echoes in Joe's mind: 'We regret that we cannot be of any assistance.' All his time and a considerable amount of money has got him nowhere. He is exploring other legal avenues but engaging solicitors is an expensive process and Joe simply does not have the money.

I am not in a financial position to engage lawyers on an ongoing basis, so I have opened an account, the Kevin Reilly Memorial Fund, to help me continue the fight. I have been pushing every way I can. I will never give up. I want the truth. I have been to counselling for my own grief and to be honest I am at my wits end. My mind is in a constant state of confusion.

I am weary from the long campaign. I still feel so much anger not just because of Kevin's death but the way the legal system has besmirched his name. The boy who killed him sent me a letter of apology, which, though I find it hard to

> accept, at least was a gesture of remorse. The
> legal system has given me nothing but one more
> insult heaped upon another.

It is easy to see, as I face Joe across a table, that he has been
much diminished by the experience of the past twelve years.
He hands me memorabilia of his slain son: the trophy for
footballer of the year, the GAA medals and a photograph. I try
to put myself in his place but I cannot, it is too painful to
contemplate bearing such a heavy and unrelenting burden.
Here in front of me are the same objects that would make any
parent proud of his son. And Joe looks back and weeps those
tears of blood, stained by thoughts of what might have been.

Joe Reilly is a decent man who has honestly toiled over his
lifetime and deserves to be enjoying the autumn of his years.
Instead they have been transformed into a continual winter of
discontent, an unbearable darkness of warped reality.

> My ex-wife and daughter are still very upset and
> they can't really get involved in the whole ins and
> outs because it is too much for them. But I will
> go on and even if I have to do everything myself
> I am determined to see justice done for my son.
> I will keep trying until the day I die. My thoughts
> and my life are consumed by nothing else.

In a booklet to coincide with a memorial day for families of
murder victims organised by Victim Support in 2002 Joe
wrote a tribute to his son.

Kevin Reilly

Ten years fighting this case,
Gross injustice done.
I would like to bring it to a close.
I want justice.
18,000 signatures collected and
given to the Department of Justice.

Time My Son's Story Was Told

I've a burning deep inside of me
It's been burning for so long for me
I can't let you go
Until I know I've set you free.

My flesh and blood
My precious son
Full of laughter
Full of fun.

It's time my son's story was told.
Remembered every day by your loving family.

One thing that Kevin Reilly in his grave will not lack is the love of his father and his family.

Injustice is a cold taskmaster with no heart and no soul and its perpetrators must know that while the bell has long tolled for a young man from Tallaght their turn will come. There may be time for redemption and it should be taken; there is no room for the wheels of bureaucracy in the cold confines of the grave.

9
DEATH OF AN
IMMIGRANT

At around 7.10 p.m. on June 21, 2000, State Pathologist Dr John Harbison received a phone call at his offices in Pearse Street, Dublin. It was from well-known Garda Detective Superintendent PJ Brown who requested that he go to an address at 94, Tyrconnell Road, Inchicore, Dublin where the body of a woman had been found. The pathologist got into his car and drove to the location, arriving at 8 p.m. There he waited for the Technical Bureau team which arrived half an hour later.

The doctor who had declared the woman dead had found the body cold which indicated that she had been dead for some time,

Dr Harbison entered the house shortly before 9 p.m., went through a hallway and into a combined sitting room and kitchenette after the video photography of the scene had been completed. He went through double glass doors to a bedroom, at the back of which was a bathroom. The end of the bedroom was taken up by a double divan bed.

On this bed lay the body of a young black woman. Her eyes were staring towards the ceiling. Her mouth was open. Both arms were stretched out with her left thumb and forefinger opposed and her right thumb between forefinger and middle finger.

Dr Harbison began his preliminary postmortem examination. He examined the neck and noted a black cloth item like a belt tightly wound around the neck. Over this was a gold chain. The upper body only was visible, the lower half being covered by a duvet. The young woman was wearing a black lace top with a black silk cummerbund. The pathologist pulled back the duvet to reveal the young woman with her legs slightly apart. She was wearing brief red lace and satin knickers.

Dr Harbison then recorded the air temperature in the room and got a reading of 19.2°C. He turned the body over and took perineal and rectal swabs. He then measured the rectal temperature which he found to be 22.8°C (approximately 14°C below normal temperature). Turning the body over enabled him to see the extremely tight and somewhat complex knotting of the belt around the neck. He concluded that it was not tied by anyone else but the victim.

The Garda search of the premises produced correspondence with a psychologist whom the victim appeared to be attending at the St Francis Psychiatric Day Hospital in north Dublin. These letters and other documents established that the victim was Ms Patricia Eddoh. It was later discovered that Patricia also had three appointments for St Brendan's Psychiatric Hospital but failed to keep any.

Dr Harbison then examined the eyes and noted a dark

smudge on the upper part of one eyeball, or possibly both – the light in the room was poor. Nevertheless he could see no sign of the true petechiae (tiny broken blood vessels) in their usual sites on the inside of the lower lids or on the lower part of the eyeball.

After the technical team had finished their work the body of the young woman was removed to the Dublin City Morgue for a full postmortem the following morning.

This was a strange and sad tale which might be better described as self murder with a strange twist.

In the late afternoon of Wednesday June 21 a woman called on Dave Griffin who owned 94, Tyrconnell Road, a house which was divided into three flats. She was a friend of Patricia Eddoh the tenant of Flat 2. She had knocked on Patricia's door and got no reply but could see the key on the inside of the door. She was concerned for Patricia's safety.

Dave Griffin had a look at the door and decided not to break in because it had a strong mortice lock. He went around the back and gained entry to the flat through the bathroom window. He found Patricia lying in her bed. He opened the door of the flat and then returned to the bed and felt her arm which was cold. He came out of the flat, locked the door and rang 999.

The fire brigade ambulance from Dolphin's Barn arrived first. Crew members Brendan Mooney and Terry O'Connor met the landlord who brought them to the room. They entered the bedroom and saw the body of the woman lying in the bed. Terry checked for a pulse but there was none and he realised she had been dead for some time. They noted that her neck was swollen and an item like a scarf was tightened around her neck.

To Brendan Mooney this sight and the fact that the victim's two arms were outstretched indicated that she might have been pinned back. They informed Sub-Officer Hurley that the woman was dead and it looked suspicious. They left the room and preserved the scene until the gardaí arrived.

Dave Griffin identified the body as Patricia Eddoh to Garda Yvonne Glacken and said that she had lived in the flat for six or eight months. She used to come to his workshop to chat and get things fixed. She was generally in good form but about a week earlier she had been acting strangely. Another tenant had said to him that she was not going out of her flat. He had visited her but she did not appear to be listening and she seemed in a trance.

The following morning after identification by Garda Glacken and the arrival of the Technical Bureau team of Detective Garda Willie Brennan, Ballistics and Detective Garda Joe McCartney, Photography, Dr Harbison began the postmortem. The woman was 5 foot 2 inches in height and weighed 132 lbs. He noted that there were four studded earrings in each ear. The body was turned over and the pathologist noted a single long blonde hair adhering to the buttocks.

There were no other injuries on the body other than a superficial scratch on the chest The internal examination revealed nothing abnormal with the exception of possible signs of a pregnancy, which also could have been explained by hormonal treatment.

After the examination was complete Dr Harbison made his three main conclusions which were:

1. Patricia Isioma Eddoh died from constriction of the neck or self-strangulation. Self-strangulation is possible when carried out by a ligature, but impossible manually. The technique, in my experience, is one of self-winding of the ligature, not very tightly, around the neck and either knotting or tying it during the period before unconsciousness supervenes.

   This is a rare finding though I can recall at least three others in the past. In two of those, the number of turns around the neck were far greater that those in the case of Miss Eddoh. I have no reason to suspect homicidal strangulation on the grounds of the deceased's bedroom and flat being locked on the inside, the owner having to force his way through a window.

2. There was an absence of any bruising or evidence of assault on the deceased.

3. There was evidence that the deceased had been receiving counselling and was in the care of a clinical psychologist for several weeks preceding her death. I am satisfied, subject to the coroner's decision, that this death was consistent with self-infliction.

Dr Harbison gave the cause of death as vagal inhibition due to self-strangulation.

So what caused this young Nigerian immigrant to murder herself in such a strange and rare manner? Who was Patricia Eddoh?

Garda Yvonne Glacken had the responsibility of providing answers to these questions and discovered in the course of her inquiry some mysterious things about the victim, including a dual identity.

Twenty-year-old Patricia Isioma Eddoh arrived in Ireland on December 10, 1998, and applied for asylum the following day. She failed to produce any documentation to confirm her identity. She lived at Leitrim House on the Upper Drumcondra Road until late 1999 when she moved into the flat on Tyrconnell Road, which was secured with the help of friends. She was receiving social welfare payments and rent allowance in her name from the Department of Social and Family Affairs.

In February 2000 she was refused asylum and she appealed the decision towards the end of the same month. No date for the appeal was set and no deportation order was issued as a result of the refusal. She had been assigned a legal representative, Thomas Kelly, for the appeal, who spoke to her several times on the telephone and sent her correspondence. He felt that she sounded anxious.

But her anxieties were hardly due to the asylum process since she was under no immediate pressure. Nor was the source financial as the Garda examination of the flat had revealed a large amount of cash.

Under the assumed name of Anita Peterson with an address at 444, South Circular Road, Dublin 8 she registered with a nursing agency and was employed as a care assistant in Carysfort Road, Blackrock, County Dublin for a year from early 1999 to early 2000. She produced a passport as identification to the agency and a London telephone number. She gave two references.

The first, it would later transpire, was a place where she had never worked and the second turned out to be an ex-boyfriend who knew her as Anita Peterson. She had asked him if she could use his name as a referee. He was prepared to say that she took care of an elderly relative for him and his family. She used his place of employment to receive faxes and to telephone home.

Her wages were paid into an account in a building society in Drumcondra. She had a good work record and was liked by colleagues, patients and her employer. She told them that she had an aunt in the South Circular Road.

But both in work and her personal life Patricia/Anita was weaving a web of deceit. Perhaps it was a burden that became too great for a woman thousands of miles away from her home in West Africa with the fear that the net might close and expose her dual identity and expose her deceit. Patricia Eddoh already had a conviction for larceny in the Dublin District Court, dating back to March 1999.

During her time in Carysfort Nursing Home, her employer heard her talking about having to mind her baby in England

and a boyfriend collected her regularly from work in a car. One night she walked out of work, saying that she had to go to England to visit her mother who was ill. This was despite efforts on the part of her employer to help her. Her mother was not ill and did not live in England.

After she walked out of Carysfort Nursing Home she worked from May 7 at Mount Tabor Nursing Home. While it appeared that Patricia Eddoh was the only tenant at her flat on Tyrconnell Road, at least two other people stayed for some periods of time and both claimed rent allowance from social welfare. One, a man, stayed for a month and then disappeared without trace.

A woman who used the address also claimed rent allowance but when gardaí searched the flat, it was obvious to them that Patricia Eddoh was the only resident. This woman stopped claiming rent allowance but was already the subject of concern by the Eastern Health Board, and a social welfare official had contacted Kilmainham Garda Station about the matter. Patricia was paying the rent charged for two people.

In the weeks leading up to her death friends, including a first cousin, members of a religious group and the caretaker, began to be worried about Patricia's erratic behaviour, withdrawing into her own world, her rambling speech and poor eating habits. They all gave statements to the gardaí for the purpose of the inquest which was held at the Dublin City Coroner's Court on March 28, 2001.

Maria Abayenimen, her cousin, arrived in Ireland almost a year after Patricia and kept in regular contact. At midnight on

June 8, 2000, she received a phone call from her cousin asking her to come to the flat. Maria explained that it was too late and that she would come over the next morning.

> I grew up with my cousin. Patricia's mother and mine are first cousins. We were good friends. We visited a lot since I came to Ireland in October 1999. When I arrived at 94 Tyrconnell Road on the morning after Patricia rang, she was not herself, she was worried. She asked me to forgive her. We didn't have a falling out. We had arguments like all friends. She had also asked her neighbour to forgive her. She refused to let me go and I stayed overnight.
>
> She complained about many things and asked me what she was going to do. She could not get a job. She felt everything was going wrong. On Sunday we both went to my house in Tallaght. We went out and she started talking again. She cried. She didn't take a shower and wouldn't eat. She drank a couple of bottles of coke.
>
> Patricia stayed with me on Sunday night and she went home on Monday evening. She said she would be fine, she would be okay. On Tuesday and Wednesday we spoke on the telephone.
>
> On Thursday Richard Ndaba [the caretaker] telephoned to say there was a problem. He said she was not herself, out of character. I

telephoned her on Thursday night. She told me her mum was dead, she had got the news. I telephoned home to Nigeria to a friend who knows and she said her mum was fine.

I telephoned Patricia back and invited her to come to my house on Sunday night to telephone Nigeria and organise her mum to be there. On Friday I called down to her flat and she would not answer the door or the telephone. Later she looked out but did not let me in. Much later, she let me in and I tried to talk to her. She was tired. I did everything to find out what was wrong with her but couldn't.

I saw a mark on her neck. The caretaker Richard Ndaba later told me that she tried to strangle herself. She said she was only messing and that it was a scratch.

She refused to go home with me or tell her mum she was okay. Early Sunday morning I called to take her down to my own house. We called her mum from my house that morning. She promised everyone everything was okay. She and I talked to her mum for one and a half hours. Her mum gave her advice and verses to read from the Bible.

She went home on Sunday night as she had a job interview the following morning. She was in good form going home. She promised to phone

the next day. She didn't call. I tried her on
Monday evening but I just got the answering
machine. I rang Richard Ndaba on Tuesday but
he had not seen her.

I got a call from Richard on Wednesday and
he asked me to come to the flat. On the evening
of Thursday June 22, I went with Garda Yvonne
Glacken to the City Morgue in Marino. At
5 p.m. I identified a female body lying there to
Garda Glacken as being that of my cousin
Patricia Eddoh.

Her friend Mojisola Odula knew Patricia for about nine
months. At one time they were going to share
accommodation but it did not work out. She considered her
friend, who was from a different part of Nigeria, as lively and
outgoing. She had not seen her for a month when, the Friday
before Patricia's death, Mojisola called to Tyrconnell Road at
2 p.m.

When I spoke to her I found her very depressed.
As a matter of fact she was rambling. She gave
me the impression that she had done something
wrong and she could not be forgiven for this.
She would not tell me what she had done. She
told me that she had sinned greatly. She kept
saying God could not help her.

She told me that she was scared to leave the
house. She did not explain why although I tried

to get her to explain. She did not seem like she was being threatened by anybody in particular. I asked if she was in trouble with the gardaí but she did not answer. I asked if she had been asked to leave the country, but she said that was a small matter.

She did not tell me anything else about this. I could not make any sense of what she was telling me. I left after some time and I contacted two pastors to go and see her. One was Pastor Tony and the other Pastor Kunle who lives with me.

Pastor Kunle, who is from Lagos, is a pastor of the Pentecostal Christian Church and preached every Sunday. After receiving the call he went to Tyrconnell Road and knocked on the door. It was opened by an African man whom he did not recognise but who was another tenant called Emmanuel Gavine.

He told me that the only reason that Patricia was depressed was that she had split up with her boyfriend two weeks before. I then knocked on Patricia's door and got no answer. Another pastor, whose name is Tony, arrived and we called out Patricia's name but she still wouldn't answer. Then the landlord arrived and tried to get her to open the door. The landlord wanted to force the door but we said to give her more time.

After twenty minutes Patricia opened the
door and we spoke to her. Pastor Tony called
another Christian lady to come and convince
Patricia to let her stay with her so she would not
be on her own. The Christian lady arrived and
the three of us prayed and talked to Patricia. She
was confused in her conversation. I stayed for
about an hour. I would see a Satanic attack and
by that I mean a spirit inside her.

She kept saying she deserved to be punished
for what she had done and deserved to die. I left
after an hour and the lady and the other pastor
stayed. I went back to see Patricia on Saturday
June 17 at about 2.30 p.m. I spoke with her and
there was no problem about opening the door.
We discussed a lot of things but I could not get
to the bottom of her depression.

Emmanuel Gavine, the other tenant, talked to her regularly.
He described her as happy with a lot of friends. Four weeks
before her death, he noticed a change.

She became very sad and seemed to be confused
and talked to herself. She appeared to be
wanting to tell something, but then wouldn't. I
don't know if she had a boyfriend but a lot of
friends used to call, both white guys and
coloured guys. She started not using the
television or the radio or electricity in the flat.

> The last time I saw Patricia was Sunday June
> 18 at about 10.30 p.m. I returned from the shops
> and when I opened my door, Patricia opened
> her door to see who it was. She looked at me but
> didn't say anything, she just banged her door.
> She looked sad. From that time I did not see
> Patricia or hear any noise from her flat.

Caretaker Richard Ndaba found Patricia a friendly, outgoing
person with loads of friends but in early June he too noticed
a change in her mood. About a week later he noticed that she
had a mark on the front of her neck.

> I asked her about the mark, she said it was
> nothing. I asked her if she did it to herself and
> she said no. She would not let me look at it. I
> telephoned her cousin that evening to tell her
> about it. Her cousin rang her but did not find
> out how the mark happened.

The following Wednesday, June 21, Mojisola Odula called
over to Tyrconnell Road between 3 p.m. and 4 p.m.

> I knocked for quite some time but she didn't
> answer. I rang all the bells but nobody came out.
> I was concerned and went to my friend's house
> in Clondalkin and while there I remembered
> that I had Patricia's landlord's number. I called
> him and explained the circumstances and that I
> was worried.

Dave Griffin, the landlord, responded immediately.

Garda Yvonne Glacken made attempts to contact Patricia's mother and family. A request followed by two reminders were sent to the Nigerian embassy and a message was left at her home in Lagos by the Red Cross. Her mother had travelled out of Lagos and could not be contacted.

No one contacted Garda Glacken up to the time of the inquest, held nine months after Patricia's death. There were tears shed for this young immigrant, but most were shed by her before her passing, tears that would be transformed by self-murder into the cold blood of death.

The answer to the mystery of why lies with the body of Patricia Eddoh in an unmarked grave on the poor ground of Glasnevin cemetery.

10
NICHOLA SWEENEY

On the evening of April 27, 2002, two young girls, Nichola Sweeney and her friend Sinead O'Leary, were alone in Nichola's house in a Cork suburb. They were full of the joys of life – until a young psychopath broke into the house. He did not know who he was going to find, but he had murder on his mind. With brutality beyond belief he murdered beautiful Nichola Sweeney who was just six months short of her twenty-first birthday. Her friend Sinead O'Leary, despite being stabbed twenty times, managed to escape. Peter Whelan got life plus fifteen years for the crime. But only a life sentence meaning life will in any way diminish the nightmare into which Nichola's parents John and Josephine were plunged.

Nichola Jayne Sweeney was born in the Bons Secours Hospital on October 6, 1981. She spent two weeks in intensive care after the birth. Her mother, Josephine, had suffered three miscarriages before Nichola was born. Her mother and father, John, were delighted with the arrival of a beautiful daughter who would enrich their lives over the next two decades.

Although Nichola was born in Cork, at the age of one the family moved to London where her father was involved in the pub trade. Over the next fifteen years she visited Ireland at least once a year. These were memorable and nostalgic trips with her parents and her younger brother, Sean. During this time she developed a great love for the country of her birth and all things Irish.

Her holidays were spent mostly in Kerry with her grandparents and relatives and she loved the rural landscape and the wild beauty of the county. She loved animals, particularly horses, and even the smallest of insects was special in her eyes. Her love of animals inspired her to be a vegetarian.

Back in London she developed her passion and went horse riding regularly. She attended St Joseph's primary and La Sainte Union secondary school, both in Highgate. Her special subjects were music and art. She was a member of the choir in St Joseph's parish church and took up Irish dancing at the local parish hall. Nichola was constantly asking her parents to move back to Ireland, emphasising how safe it was compared to London. A house with land situated opposite an equestrian centre came on the market in Cork.

Underwood House was in every sense a dream home. Perched on a hillside overlooking the harbour and Hop Island, it was a sylvan setting with eight neighbours. It could have been in the middle of the countryside but yet was only five miles from Cork city centre. Nichola took an instant liking to the house and persuaded her parents to buy it. It was a fateful decision.

Nichola attended Scoil Mhuire in the city centre, where

she sat her Leaving Cert. She was a happy, loving daughter and despite the fact that she was from a comfortable background, her parents had always emphasised the importance of real family values. Nichola took this on board, thus the presence of spiritual and moral values in her lifestyle.

She was an intelligent, well-balanced and creative young woman who had a lot to offer the world.

On the evening of Saturday April 27, 2002, Nichola Sweeney arrived back at her home in Rochestown from her part-time job in Brown's Café in the Brown Thomas department store in Cork city centre. Earlier she had said goodbye to her work colleagues, adding that she would see them the following day.

It was 7 p.m. and normally her parents who owned and ran four pubs in London would be home for the weekend. But this time they had stayed on with her little brother, four-year-old Christopher. Her younger brother Sean was still at work at his part-time job at the nearby Maryborough House Hotel. She, as usual, phoned John and Josephine and spent ten minutes in conversation. She said that she would ring them back later.

Her friend Sinead O'Leary was calling over. They planned to cook a meal, study for upcoming exams and watch a video that Sinead had hired. After Sinead arrived, they ate and sat down to study. Sean arrived home then and they relaxed and conversed happily.

In the nearby Rochestown Inn three young men with a reputation for trouble were sowing the seeds for what one of them would translate into unimaginable evil. Barry Dolan, Stacy McCarthy and Peter Whelan were well known to the gardaí. Whelan was a neighbour of the Sweeney family but entirely unknown to them. The twenty-year-old had a history of dysfunctional and violent behaviour. Three months earlier he had been involved in an assault while in the company of Dolan. At a New Year's Eve party the thugs attacked the party-goers with hurleys and bottles. Whelan was already portraying his psychopathic tendencies, his rage against the world an antidote to his low self-esteem.

The three were causing trouble in the pub and the barman decided to stop serving them. As the barman turned his back Whelan picked up an ashtray and was going to strike him on the head, but the barman turned and avoided him. The gardaí were called but no arrest was made – the young men were asked to leave. Whelan was made aware that a summons for the attack at the party was being delivered to his home that evening.

Barry Dolan went home leaving Stacy McCarthy and Whelan to go their own way. McCarthy got a lift and Whelan was left alone, walking home behind a young man. He later admitted that he intended to kill him. He decided to go home and get two knives to do the job. When he got home, he was given the summons. This delayed him and when he went back out on the road the young man had disappeared. But Whelan was murderous; someone had to pay for his life being screwed up.

He was passing the entrance to the Sweeney home and

decided to go in over the high wall. He circled the house until he found the unlocked back door.

Shortly before, Nichola and Sinead had been phoned by friends who had asked them to go out and socialise. They went up to Nichola's room to change. Her brother Sean's friend Conor called and since the girls were going out Sean decided to join Conor at his house. He asked the girls if they wanted a lift but Nichola said that she had already ordered a taxi. He left at 10.45 p.m.

Ten minutes later the girls were almost ready. Nichola was in her en-suite bathroom, finishing her make-up. Sinead was curling her hair, sitting on the bed.

Suddenly a man appeared at the open door. He walked towards Sinead and, with a flurry of punches, knocked her to the ground. Working himself to a frenzy he started to kick and stamp on her. Nichola, hearing the noise, came out of the bathroom. Whelan pulled out the two knives and began stabbing Sinead.

Nichola, on the other side of the bed, begged him to stop. His eyes were now totally focused on her. He smiled, and the evil grin transformed his face into an image of his evil mind. Suddenly he lunged at Nichola.

Sinead had been stabbed twenty times but despite horrific injuries, no vital organ had been punctured. She managed to escape downstairs, slipping constantly in her own blood, and locked herself in a bathroom where she called for help on her mobile phone. She had to grope blindly in the darkness because Whelan had turned out the lights as he'd made his way through the house. This is a classic act of a psychopath on a murder spree. Hickock and Smith, who murdered a whole family in their house in the American mid-west in 1959, did exactly the same.

There is little doubt that Nichola's intervention saved her friend's life but she paid with her own. Whelan savagely stabbed her again and again until he penetrated her heart. The monster then went in search of Sinead, but his own act of turning off the lights frustrated him and, deciding not to hang about, he left the house through the front door, a trail of bloody human destruction behind him.

He went back home, changed his bloodstained clothes, hid them and washed his hands. Then, upon seeing the gardaí at Underwood House, he went to his uncle's house next door and they both joined the crowd on the drive of the Sweeney home. Whelan was acting the role of a concerned neighbour. In the wake of his horrendous brutality this was an act of utter callousness.

But Sinead had survived and was able to give a perfect description of the attacker who at that time was on the driveway, as calm and composed as any of the other onlookers who had no knowledge of the terror and evil he had dispensed inside the house. But the mask of evil did slip. When confronted by gardaí he remarked, 'I am sorry I didn't do more.'

The dream home that is Underwood House rests on top of a hill, and a winding, descending driveway leads to the road outside. To the left is the Whelan household. Not a great distance from the Sweeney's front door the roof of the house where the killer of their daughter lived is visible. Nichola's parents' grief has been intensified by the fact that Whelan's parents have never offered one word of sympathy or condolence since the murder. John says they cannot understand this.

> Peter Whelan pleaded guilty shortly before the trial began. It is not as if there is any doubt about the case. He killed our daughter and tried to kill her friend Sinead. When he was questioned by the gardaí he said he was sorry he had not killed more.
>
> Some people ask us how did we not recognise the evil in him. I had passed him a number of times and he seemed distant but polite. There was no way of telling what a monster he grew to be.

John and Josephine Sweeney grew up in County Kerry and both came from modest backgrounds. They emigrated young and built up a considerable business in London owning three pubs and a nightclub. This was gained as Josephine puts it through 'years of hard work'. But now she says since Nichola's death it does not matter. For all the years of toil this is the reward.

Their grief is further deepened by the coincidences that conspired on the night to lead Whelan to their door. When he was ejected with Dolan and McCarthy from Rochestown Inn they went to Dolan's house. Dolan's mother did not want the others there however, as she was aware they had been asked to leave the pub. 'One got a lift and Whelan was left on his own,' says John.

> He saw another young man in front of him on the road and decided to kill him. He went home to get the knives but the summons was waiting for him and this delayed him. When he got back out the young man was gone. He then turned to our house.

> He first tried the front door but it was locked and he went to the back door which unfortunately was not and he let himself in. My son Sean had just gone out. Whelan had the knives hidden and we think that if there were other people in the house, he would have pretended that he had wandered in looking for his dog or otherwise. But that was not to be.

John brings myself and photographer Mike McSweeney along the route which Whelan took, through the corridor that stretches the length of the house and up the stairs onto another corridor that led to Nichola's bedroom. Nothing has changed in the room, except of course a new carpet to replace the bloodstained one. John points out where Sinead was sitting on the side of the bed when Whelan appeared at the doorway.

> Whelan started punching and kicking Sinead

and then produced the knives from under his
hoodie. He stabbed Sinead with one of the
knives, breaking it on her with the ferocity of the
attack. When Nichola came out of the bathroom
and pleaded with him to stop he never kept his
eyes off her. He then lunged for her. She ran
back into the bathroom but he kicked the door
in and started stabbing her with another knife.
She tried to get out of the window but he pulled
her back and stabbed her to death.

John points to the floor beside the bed where he and
Josephine's only daughter died. It is heartbreaking and
impossible that anyone could get over such a tragic and
traumatic event. People ask them how they can continue to
live in the house but John says that although it is sometimes a
problem, Nichola loved the house. The house did not harm
her and in a sense it keeps them close to the memory of
Nichola.

But the ghastly and tragic loss never goes away.

Earlier John tells me of his wife's grief, of going to the
grave in Beaufort in the early hours of the morning crying.
The pain is etched on Josephine's pretty features. The only
thing that keeps her going, she says, is her young six-year-old
son Christopher. He adored Nichola and the first thing he did
every morning was to run into her bed and cuddle her.

He keeps me going, but grief is very strange
because it seems to get worse as time goes on

and as the realities begin to become clearer.

They have set up the Nichola Sweeney foundation. The foundation is there to keep Nichola's memory alive and to give expression to her parents' fear of a monster such as Peter Whelan ever being released to perpetrate a similar crime. Full details can be had by accessing the website, www.nicholasweeneyfoundation.org

There was nothing mad about what Whelan did, and people who say he must have been mad are wrong. Whelan had a lust to kill that night. He had a previous record of violence. He is an evil psychopath who should never see the light of day. He has never shown one ounce of remorse for what he did. All he said to the gardaí was that he was 'sorry he had not killed more'.

John and indeed many experts agree that a psychopath will not change and if released will kill again. The authorities should ensure that the evil monster Peter Whelan is never given that chance. He should be left in prison – the only just reward for the savage and merciless murder of a beautiful, caring and loving young woman.

11
A COLD-BLOODED MURDER

In the springtime of Life Catherine was like a
    beautiful flower, so untimely cut down.
What ache fills our heart today as we mourn her
    passing.
She exuded the full exuberance of youth,
Her laughter lit up the lives of her family,
    friends and workmates,
While the warmth of her smile and her words
    burned into our memory.
She was lighthearted, fun loving, good-natured,
    wholesome and humorous.
Her world was untouched by the more sinister
    things of life,
Peace exuded from her presence,
Yet what she achieved in time, her little acts of
    kindness and love are the real stuff of life,
Her innocence is a proof to duplicity,
Her unquestioning trust showed a freedom
    never to be experienced by those who deceive.
In the Garden of Paradise may she be arrayed
    in splendour,

May her virtues be rewarded with everlasting
  bliss,
May she look on us who mourn her, as she
  always did with
Love and trust and with a smile.

Tribute to Catherine Kealy

At half past midnight on May 1, 1992, State Pathologist Dr John Harbison was contacted by Garda Communications and informed that the body of a girl had been found in a car park in Thurles, County Tipperary. It was suspected that she had been murdered. Dr Harbison drove to Thurles, arriving at the scene of the crime at 1.30 in the morning. There he observed the body of a woman covered by a plastic sheet, which he removed.

Superintendent Peter Griffin of Thurles Garda Station, who accompanied him to the scene, told the pathologist that the deceased had been rolled over on to her back when found in the hopes that she could be resuscitated. There had been heavy rainfall and the woman lay on the edge of a large puddle. Her trousers were pulled down to expose the lower abdomen and hip area.

Rigor mortis was established throughout the body except in the left arm. Dr Harbison took the temperature of the body, which was 17.7°C, 20° below normal body temperature. The ambient temperature was 12.5°C. When he completed his examination at the scene, the body was wrapped in plastic sheeting and removed to Nenagh District Hospital for the full postmortem examination.

Dr Harbison noted in his postmortem report that the body was that of a young woman, 5 foot 3 inches in height, with short, light brown hair. There was a crop of petechial haemorrhages on the right side of the forehead, extending down over the right temple. Petechial haemorrhages in both eyes were evident, particularly on the inner surfaces of the lower lids. He noted that the fingernails were so badly bitten that he could not recover any scrapings. There were small cuts on both sides of the forehead, bruises near the right eyebrow, on the bridge of the nose and along both sides, and over the lower jaw under the right ear. There were small cuts over the left side of the chin and right cheek, probably sustained from contact with gravel on the ground.

On the left side of the neck there was a patterned bruise, which was the imprint of the neckband of her jumper. There was a group of small cuts on the front of the neck over the Adam's apple. Two bruises, each three quarters of an inch across, showed on the right side of the neck. There was a bruise on the little finger side of the right wrist. There were cuts on the thighs and on the inner side of the right knee.

The back and right side of the head as well as the outer surface of the brain had evidence of bleeding. Internal examination of the neck also revealed bleeding and a large haemorrhage over the larynx. The rest of the internal examination revealed no injuries or disease in the major organs, which were those of a healthy individual. No evidence of sexual assault was found.

Dr John Harbison's postmortem conclusions were:

1. The deceased, Catherine Kealy, in my opinion died of asphyxia due to strangulation. The degree of injury to the neck was not great and from the distribution of bruising and abrasion on the overlying skin, I am of the impression that pressure was exerted on the thyroid cartilage, on the cricoid cartilage below and on the upper trachea. In a young girl this age these flexible cartilaginous structures can be compressed against the spine behind without structural damage, that is without fracture.

2. The degree of injury on the deceased's face and neck was not marked. Particularly, the neck was free of injury on both sides. This suggested that death supervened fairly quickly, although the abundant asphyxial or petechial haemorrhages in the eyes indicated that death was asphyxial rather than due to vagal inhibition.

3. Some bleeding of the traumatic type was present on the left side of the brain. There was some bruising of the scalp and right side of the head and there were abrasions on the left side of the forehead. This grouping of

injuries could have been caused by forcing Catherine's face downwards against hard ground. The presence of some grit in the larynx or airway, like that seen on the ground beside her body, would lend credence to such a manoeuvre having taken place.

4. Examination of the vulva showed blood loss consistent with menstruation, as no genital injuries were found to explain it. There were no injuries to suggest sexual assault.

5. Catherine was a healthy girl at the time of her death.

6. Assessment of rigor mortis and measurement of air and body temperatures, were consistent with death having taken place around the middle of the previous night.

On the night of the murder Superintendent Peter Griffin took charge of the investigation into the circumstances of the death. He was brought to a Garda patrol car where a twenty-five-year-old man, Anthony Kiely, was seated. He had been arrested as a suspect for the killing of the girl. Superintendent Peter Griffin later saw Kiely, who appeared to be in a state of distress, in Thurles Garda Station and arranged for him to be seen by a doctor.

At 1 a.m. he returned to the car park with a local woman, Mrs Mary Mulcahy, who identified the body as that of twenty-two-year-old Catherine Kealy of Conlon's Road, Nenagh, an employee of Hayes Hotel in Thurles.

Supt Griffin then ordered the detention of Anthony Kiely for questioning in relation to the murder of Catherine Kealy who, Kiely claimed, was his girlfriend since the previous October. The following day Kiely admitted the manslaughter of Catherine.

The twenty-five-year-old said that he had been drinking all that day in Tullamore and that evening returned to Thurles where he continued drinking. He rang Catherine at Hayes Hotel and she joined him in the pub after she finished her shift at 10 p.m. They went to the car park to make love. He began caressing her neck and then 'all of a sudden' started choking her. She tried to stop him and began to struggle. Catherine fell to the ground with Kiely on top of her still gripping her neck. He then lifted her head and realised that she was dead. 'I have no idea why I killed her. I didn't set out to do it and I'm really sorry it happened,' he later told gardaí. He then phoned his uncle who later reported that his nephew seemed excited and told him, 'I've killed somebody. I killed her. I killed her.'

His uncle accompanied by his wife drove to meet Kiely at Liberty Square in Thurles where he showed them the body of the young woman. He had already rung for an ambulance and the gardaí who then arrived at the scene. Kiely told them, 'I killed her, lads. I choked her.' The gardaí cautioned and arrested him. Kiely subsequently admitted manslaughter but the State refused that plea and he was charged and subsequently convicted of murder in the Central Criminal Court in Dublin.

That conviction, by definition, meant that Kiely had intent to kill and the killing was not, as he described it, some sort of bizarre accident, but rather, as prosecuting counsel Kenneth Mills S.C. described, 'bizarre and wanton'. Kiely emphasised the fact that he was drinking all day and claimed that he had some sort of blackout.

The tactic of pleading temporary insanity backfired for Kiely in advance of the trial when two independent psychiatric evaluations proved that he was sane in every sense. Which confirmed exactly what the prosecution contended, that on that fateful day Kiely had murder on his mind. And probably sex.

He claimed that he and his girlfriend had left the pub 'to make love'. It was a cold April night. Kiely, by his own admission, had a lot to drink and Catherine Kealy was most unlikely to agree to such a scenario. First of all she was a solid girl from a very respectable background who would hardly be found having sex with a drunk in a pub car park. Secondly, even if she had been disposed to engaging in sex, she would have been discouraged by the fact that she was having a period.

The drink that Kiely had ordered for her remained on the table, untouched. Are we to believe that at the mention of sex the young woman, who had just come off her shift at a very well-known Thurles hotel, would leap up from the table and abandon the warmth of the pub on the invitation of a drunk?

Apart from all that Catherine Kealy was a virgin. Kiely was seriously misguided to peddle the story of 'making love'.

The story is a figment of the diseased imagination of a man trying to cover up a far more dangerous motive. At the same time he sullies the reputation of a young woman whom he described as his girlfriend yet who, amazingly, never mentioned his name to her family.

What is far more likely is that, having managed to get Catherine to the pub, he then lured her outside, possibly by pretending he felt unwell. Since her trousers had been pulled down over her hips, Kiely obviously made a botched attempt at sexual contact – nothing like 'caressing her neck'. When she resisted him, he viciously and cold-bloodedly strangled Catherine Kealy and extinguished a young life forever.

This merciless action has literally ruined the lives of Catherine's parents, Donal and Joan, whose health deteriorated in the aftermath to such an extent that Joan is now an invalid, spending long periods in hospital.

Ironically, Donal was a leading member of the Legal Justice Action group which campaigned for many years for reform of the justice system. The murder of his daughter illustrated just how inadequate that system is and since then he has been a vocal critic of a system that he says does not take the victim or relatives into account but looks after the perpetrator at every turn.

> When a member of the Garda and a local priest arrived at our house at around three in the morning to tell us that Catherine had been

killed we began to live the worst nightmare that any parents can imagine. I never thought that the State Pathologist Dr John Harbison would arrive in our neighbourhood, least of all to examine my daughter.

It is something that you never get over but it would be much easier to bear if a life sentence for the murder meant just that. But it does not; it can mean anything. Anthony Kiely could be walking the streets any day now. We are the ones that have got the life sentence.

The grieving Kealy family were shocked and angered when in May of 2002 a picture of Anthony Kiely appeared in *The Sunday World* walking through the streets of Dublin, listening to his walkman and a cigarette in his hand. There was no prison officer in sight. The convicted murderer was apparently on his way to a daily cookery course. It also emerged that Kiely had been given temporary release at Christmas and Easter.

Donal was devastated.

When the judge said life, I presumed that it meant life but I was told afterwards that life can mean just seven years. Kiely had served ten years at the time and was now being prepared for release. I come from a very Christian family and I am very forgiving, but the murder of Catherine is one thing that I could never forgive.

Donal did some investigating through an inside prison contact and learned that Kiely was being held in the training unit in Mountjoy where he was not only allowed out to do a course and for holidays, but also had been let out at weekends. Donal and his family were terrified at the thought of bumping into the cruel killer of their daughter in Thurles, Kiely's hometown.

Donal also learned that Kiely had been attending Bible readings with the Quakers giving the impression that he had found God and was on the way to rehabilitation.

Contact was made with me with the suggestion that I might meet with a member of the Quaker group. This I interpreted as a move to offer the hand of forgiveness to Kiely.

That will never happen and I refused to meet anyone who had anything to do with Kiely. He showed no mercy to Catherine and has never expressed one ounce of remorse for his actions. In fact . . . he did not even have the decency to the tell the truth about what happened but lied again and again. He might be fooling the authorities and the Quakers but he will never fool me.

I can't sleep at night; I hear my daughter screaming for help. If Catherine had died a normal death, you would get over it. If it was a car accident, you could say that the person did not mean it. But there is a big difference

between murder and an accident. It is quite
obvious the authorities who have sanctioned
Kiely's release do not appreciate this fact.

Donal Kealy and his family have absolutely no faith in the
Department of Justice, and his pleas to previous Ministers for
Justice have fallen on deaf ears. He realises, in common with
other relatives of murder victims, that they have no status or
influence within the system and the extent of their suffering
is not taken into account by either the Minister for Justice
who has discretion in the matter of remission and release, or
the members of the parole board.

Donal managed to have the then Justice Minister John
O'Donoghue confronted in the dáil on the issue through
questions tabled by Fine Gael TDs Alan Shatter and Brian
Hayes.

O'Donoghue explained his policy in relation to temporary
release and parole:

I have explained to the House on several
occasions recently that temporary release or
parole is a feature of prison systems worldwide
and it is an important vehicle for reintegrating
offenders into the community in a planned and
controlled way. There is, undoubtedly, a
significant element of risk in this which requires
careful consideration, and paramount concern is
the safety of the public. However it falls to me as
minister to strike a balance between sometimes

conflicting considerations, such as the rehabilitation of the offender and his reintegration into the community and any risk which a particular release might pose.

In making individual decisions on temporary release, particularly in cases involving the death of a victim or other serious offences, the possible effect on victims or their families is an extremely important consideration. To address these concerns, conditions can be imposed on temporary releases in relation to where the offender may go. Such conditions are attached expressly in view of the distress that encountering an offender may cause. In this case a prohibition on travel to the area where the victim's family resides has been applied and will continue to apply in view of the strong concerns expressed to me.

The case will remain under regular review and progress will be closely monitored. It is my intention to continue a programme of temporary release in respect of this prisoner, subject to ongoing review and continued good behaviour.

O'Donoghue promised to inform the Kealy family of significant changes in the administration of the sentence of Kiely which would include notice of temporary release programmes.

It was suggested to the minister that, in many instances, the notification to the victim's family is grossly inadequate and his reply confirmed everything that Donal Kealy had feared and complained about in relation to the treatment of Anthony Kiely as compared to his family.

> In relation to this prisoner, who was convicted for murder, sentenced to life imprisonment and has served in the region of ten years, the arrangements in place, which are part of the rehabilitative process of the prisoner, are not of a nature that would require them to be communicated to the victim's family. These arrangements at all times take into account the effect such a release can have on the community and on the family of the victim.
>
> Specifically, the prisoner is allowed temporary release under supervision to attend a work-training programme. He is not allowed, during a period of temporary release, to be anywhere in the vicinity of the place where the offence took place or in the region where the family resides.
>
> The prisoner has not breached any of the terms of his temporary release. The Sentence Review Group has reviewed the case twice to date and is satisfied with the progress of the prisoner in prison. Advice from all other authorities is taken into account.

This statement when put in the context of the cold-hearted and vicious murder of Catherine Kealy beggars belief. The minister would have the family of the victim be in some way grateful for the fact that Kiely when he is let out is not allowed go to Thurles or Nenagh. That these arrangements of release should not be communicated to the family is downright cruelty when instead they are faced with the horror of finding out about them in the pages of a newspaper.

The review group, the minister says, is happy with the progress of Kiely in prison. How much is the review group familiar with the details of his crime and the effects it has had on the family? A father who relives the nightmare of his daughter's killing every night and a mother who has become an invalid is the tragic aftermath of such a crime. Killers murder more than their victims.

Is the group aware of the manipulative nature of sex offenders and killers? Experts at fooling the authorities, they then go on to commit more crimes – including murder – on their release.

The group is sanctioning the release of a killer who lied in his statement about the reason for the crime and at the same time besmirched the reputation of his victim in a disgraceful and self-serving manner.

This is a man in whom the Sentence Review Group placed a certain amount of trust. At least on one occasion Kiely proved that this trust was misplaced. While given weekend temporary release he was supposed to stay with a nominated person who filled the role of supervisor. He in fact did not stay where he was supposed to and, instead of returning on Sunday night, did not appear until Monday.

The Sentence Review Group does not impress the victim's father.

> Clearly the group has ignored one of the guidelines in determining the decision to let Kiely out on temporary release – the nature of the offence committed should take the experience of the victim's family into account. Does the group know how much we as a family have suffered at the hands of Kiely? If they don't they should.

> Here they are giving a killer privileges while the family get none. Our lives have been ruined by Kiely, and a bunch of do-gooders are trying to make his life as comfortable as possible. That is not justice for us or our daughter.

Obviously there are cases where criminals express remorse for their actions and are worthy of rehabilitation, but judging by the nature of his killing of Catherine Kealy, his subsequent lying, his lack of remorse and flouting of the terms of his temporary release, Anthony Kiely does not deserve to be in that category.

For Donal Kealy and his family the stark fact remains, they will never see their beloved daughter and sister again but, if the present trend continues, could well see her killer on the streets of Thurles.

Her long-suffering father said that he would never have opened his mouth about the case if a life sentence for murder in this country meant exactly that. He would have got on with his life and his grief. But he has been so traumatised by the absence of real mandatory sentencing, he would be in favour of bringing back capital punishment.

It is an extreme position for a civilised and intelligent man to take, but under the circumstances of the brutal murder of his daughter, entirely understandable.

12
BEYOND BELIEF

In July 1982 Lorraine was born, the beautiful new life of the little girl who was my daughter and who was to become my best friend over her nineteen years. As I held her little hand and took her to school in The Holy Family in Ennis for the first time, I felt this was Lorraine's first step into the future and I wished with all my heart that it would be a good one.

She danced and sang her way through life, winning many awards for Irish dancing along the way. Lorraine was a kind and gentle person. She always took other people's problems on board and felt sorry for anyone she thought had anything less than herself. She loved life but always said the world was a very unfair place.

She was very close to both her older brother Derrick and younger brother Daragh whom she helped out with homework and anything he had difficulty in doing. He loved the lively atmosphere that Lorraine brought to the house. For Derrick, when she worked in his bar, she was a rock of reliability, loyalty and honesty.

She was a loving and beautiful human being who had everything in life to look forward to. The abominable cruelty of one man would put that beyond her tender grasp. This little girl I gave life to and loved so dearly was taken and a large part of us all went with her.

Lorraine's favourite bedtime story as a little girl was Sleeping Beauty. I read the story time and time again until she was old enough to read it herself. Just like the princess she grew up to be beautiful, wise, friendly and well behaved. Everyone who knew her, loved her. As I sat beside the casket in which Lorraine lay, in the midst of my anguish and pain this story kept flashing in front of me. Lorraine will always be my daughter, my best friend and my Sleeping Beauty. I hope some day I will meet her again, in a place where there will be no more sadness or pain.

Ann O'Connor

Unfortunately for Lorraine there was no prince to give her the kiss of life and happiness but an evil monster whose poisonous lips and mind sucked the very last breath from her body.

I met Ann O'Connor and her son Derrick in the darkened interior of the pub they run, McCarthy's bar in Ennis. For over two hours they related the horrendous story of the murder of a daughter and sister. They are still in a living nightmare. That evening I returned to my room in the Old Ground Hotel and after going asleep experienced flashbacks to the detail of the murder in a manner that I had never experienced before.

What haunted me was not just the murder and the vile detail of the killer's defiling of the body but the terrible realisation that this tragedy, in the lead up, was just like the murder in 2002 of the two ten-year-olds, Holly Wells and Jessica Chapman, in Soham. Had events been properly monitored, it need never have happened. The killer of Lorraine O'Connor, Noel Hogan, is the Ian Huntley of Ireland.

On the night of Saturday, October 20, 2001, Ann O'Connor was finishing a busy night in McCarthy's pub in Market Street. Behind the bar, frequented at the weekend by a young crowd, were Ann's daughter, nineteen-year-old Lorraine, and her boyfriend Noel Hogan, who was ten years older than her. At that particular stage of life this is a large age gap but Hogan had been going out with Lorraine since she was sixteen and the family had grudgingly accepted their daughter's choice.

For this period of time Hogan, like Huntley, was hanging around with schoolgirls. While the O'Connors may have thought this odd, they are not experts in psychology and could not detect any sign that Hogan was a wolf in sheep's clothing. And they had no knowledge of Hogan's history, which should have been an open book.

In their midst was a dangerous psychopath with cruel and perverted sexual urges to maim and inflict pain on the opposite sex. He was also a master manipulator who could assume the disguise of respectability without even a hint of the evil currents flowing in his mind.

It was known to the family that Hogan was from a rough part of Limerick and came from a disadvantaged background. Typically, Lorraine would feel sorry for someone less well off than herself. Hogan would cunningly curry such sympathy. While working in a bar frequented on occasions by teenage girls, he would spin them a story that he had not got long to live because he was suffering from terminal cancer.

It was a cold and calculated lie designed to draw sympathetic attention to him and, unfortunately, it worked. In other areas of his life he was inept and, like Huntley, could not hold down a job for very long. The O'Connors gave him a job in their bar and a place at their family table and, ultimately, in the winter of 2001 a flat.

In the early hours of Sunday, October 21, Ann O'Connor was finishing up when Lorraine, who was in good form, told her mother that Hogan and herself were going to the Queen's nightclub. Lorraine asked Ann for a lift because it might be difficult to get a taxi. She also said that for the same reason she would probably stay in the spare room in Hogan's flat. Ann had noticed that Hogan was quiet that evening as if he had something on his mind.

On the same night Seamus Ball, a factory worker from Ennis, had been acting as DJ in McCarthy's pub, a task he performed at the weekends. He lived in the flat owned by Michael and Ann O'Connor on the corner of Fergus Row and

Brewer Lane which Hogan was due to share. He had spent the previous five weeks in the flat alone. He left the pub at the same time as Ann, Hogan and Lorraine, in the company of two girls he knew. They went back to the flat for drinks.

Ann, meantime, dropped the couple outside the nightclub and kissed her daughter goodnight. Again she noticed that Hogan was in a sombre mood.

Ball and his friends were only in the flat five minutes when Hogan and Lorraine arrived, explaining that they could not get into the nightclub because the doors were shut. They played CDs, drank and talked. He noticed that Lorraine was in good form but Hogan was quiet. Other than that he did not notice anything unusual. The two other girls left at 3.30 a.m.

Seamus Ball was not really listening to the conversation but thought he heard Lorraine saying 'I love you' to Hogan and he replying that he loved her too. In the latter case this would prove to be a cynical lie, typical of his life as a spinner of deceit.

They were all sitting on his bed when Seamus began to doze off. He left the flat at about 4.30 a.m. and walked to his parents' home. Since Seamus lived in the flat there is no logical reason why he left other than he was asked to by Hogan.

When Ann got up on Sunday morning, Lorraine had not returned home but this was not an unusual occurrence, so there was no cause for worry. She made her way to McCarthy's bar to prepare for the huge breakfast trade, traditional in the bar on Sunday morning. Hogan was due in at 10 a.m. but he arrived fifteen minutes late. He was, apparently, in good form and full of chat, in contrast to the last time Ann had seen him. She did not know it, but Hogan was on a high.

> He told me that Lorraine was back at the flat and would be in later. About fifteen minutes later he asked to borrow the keys of my car to go to the family house to collect a bag of washing he wanted to bring back to the flat. I thought nothing of this and told him to go ahead. Normally on a Sunday morning my husband, Michael, would be out but on this occasion a friend had called over and they were chatting over a cup of tea. My younger son Darragh was in bed upstairs.
>
> Hogan arrived at the house and greeted my husband and his friend. Everything seemed to be normal. He was collecting a few belongings and, at one stage, took out a top and ironed it. He spent about twenty minutes in the house and then drove off. We were very busy back at the bar and I did not feel the time passing. About an hour after he had gone, I noticed that the keys to the safe were missing.
>
> I rang Lorraine's phone but it was dead. I then phoned Hogan's but it was switched off. Lorraine's aunt and godmother, Mary, was there helping out. At about twelve o'clock I began to

> shiver and a dreadful feeling came over me. I
> was so close to my daughter. She would have
> rung me long ago by this stage. I knew that
> something awful had happened. I told Mary that
> Lorraine was dead. I started to scream the place
> down. I was crying and hysterical.

It was soon established that Hogan had taken flight and had stolen over €4,000 from the safe. Ann then realised that the purpose of his visit to the family home was not just to collect his belongings. Upstairs in her bedroom was the rest of the weekend takings, amounting to almost €13,000. Had Michael not been there, Hogan would have had plenty of money to tide him over. He was due in again at 8 p.m. that evening and when he did not appear Ann contacted the gardaí.

When they arrived she asked them to search Hogan's flat; Lorraine's body had to be there. At this stage the gardaí were thinking of the possibility that Lorraine may have eloped with Hogan and perhaps Ann was just another distraught and hysterical mother who after all had last seen her daughter less than twenty-four hours before. But Ann was so close to her daughter that she knew differently.

She was later informed that the flat had been searched and everything was in order. The focus would be on tracing her car and establishing if Lorraine was with Hogan and was safe or not. Sometimes instinct is a far more accurate guide than procedure.

On Monday Ann rang her son Derrick, who was on holiday

in Lanzarote with his girlfriend Helen, and he made arrangements to fly back immediately. When he arrived home he contacted Pat Kirby, a high-ranking security man in Shannon airport, who agreed to help trace Ann's car. Derrick was clear about his feelings for his sister's boyfriend.

> I never liked Hogan from the first time I met him. There were a couple of occasions when I came close to confronting him physically but in deference to Lorraine I did not do anything, something which I deeply regret now.

The next day, Tuesday, Derrick's suspicions about Hogan led him to go with his uncle to the flat in Brewery Lane to search it. One of the bedrooms had a bed with a split base comprised of two halves. Derrick pulled away the mattress and moved one half. To this day he does not know why he did not do the same to the other. 'Something told me not to,' he said.

Later he received a phone call to tell him that his security contact had tracked down Ann's car which was in a car park at Cork Airport. He was asked, along with his father, to accompany a Garda patrol car from Ennis to search the car in Cork. There was the possibility, if she was not alive, that Lorraine's body could have been concealed in the boot of the car. The Garda car left Ennis at 7.15 p.m.

A short while before, Seamus Ball, having finished work in the factory was in The Tattoo Parlour in Parnell Street. It was about 5.45 p.m.

> I was there about ten minutes and I asked Tadhg

Kelly who works in the tattoo shop to come to the flat for a look because I had spoken to him before about doing up the flat and he was going to do some Chinese designs on the wall.

Tadhg came up to the flat with me. I asked Tadhg if he would give me a hand to move the beds in the flat. The base of my bed was practically rotten, so I said I might as well use the base from Noel's room. I brought the first base from the front room into my room.

I rang my girlfriend Aoife and I was talking to her for a while. When I finished talking to Aoife I went into the front bedroom to get the second base.

I lifted up the base and a mass of heat hit me in the face and I saw blonde hair on the floor. I could see a head and a red top and I dropped the base and ran out of the room. I was panicking and I tried to ring Garda Brendan Ruane but the phone was ringing and there was no answer.

I went back to the room to make sure of what I saw. I lifted the base and I felt the heat in my face again. I saw a body on the floor. I knew it was Lorraine O'Connor. I dropped the base and ran to the Garda station.

Inspector Tom Kennedy was on duty at Ennis Garda Station

and was aware that the car in which Noel Hogan was travelling had been discovered at Cork Airport. He was informed that Seamus Ball was at the station and had discovered Lorraine O'Connor's body.

> I went to the apartment at 1 Fergus Row with Detective Gardaí Duffy, Fahy and Harrington. I was present in the room when Detectives Duffy and Fahy lifted the bed base and I observed the body of a female concealed there. I now know the body was that of Lorraine O'Connor. She was wearing a red top with black trousers. I saw a blood stain on the floor underneath her lower back and I saw marks on her neck.

Meanwhile the patrol car in which Derrick and Michael O'Connor were travelling had reached Charleville forty miles away when two mobile phones began to ring. One of the officers informed them that they were returning to Ennis Garda Station. Derrick instantly feared the worst.

> The mobiles were ringing continuously on the way back. I asked had Lorraine's body been found. I was told that I might be right but it was not confirmed to me . . . Then the lights and siren were turned on. That was confirmation for me. I was overcome by a feeling of disbelief. All this in a car with the lights flashing and the sound of siren.

The sense of unreality would be shattered by the confirmation at 9.15 p.m. that Lorraine's body had been found. Relations and friends began to gather at Ann and Michael's house. The shock was bad enough but when they discovered where she had been found there was a sense of total disbelief and anger that the flat had been searched but the body had not been found.

At Lorraine's parents' house there were scenes of abject grief. Relations and friends were screaming and crying and, as the word spread, more and more people arrived to support the family who were in a state of shock and bleak desolation. And they were angry and full of guilt because it was now clear that the killer was Noel Hogan whom the family had given a position of trust. He had rewarded them by murdering their only daughter and sister and robbing money to make good his escape.

Meanwhile the wheels of a normal murder investigation were beginning to turn. The scene was preserved and technical and forensic experts began their work. The State Pathologist's office was contacted and the then Deputy State Pathologist, Dr Marie Cassidy, was assigned to the case. The following morning she travelled to Ennis and before the postmortem made her preliminary examination at the flat.

Identification
The body was identified to me by Garda Michael McNamara of Ennis Garda Station as that of Lorraine O'Connor, d.o.b. 12/7/82 of

9 Showgrounds View, Ennis.

The body of this young female had been found the previous evening. The apartment was on several levels and the body was found on the upper level, in one of the rooms that was being used as a bedroom. Her body was enclosed in the base of the bed which had now been moved to expose the body. She was face up, her arms and legs flexed and bent. She was fully clothed. There was congestion of the face and petechiae were noted on the face and inside the eyelids. There were some marks on her neck. There was dried blood under her body, which appeared to be coming from the lower part of her body. There were no obvious bleeding injuries, although the clothing covering the lower part of the body was not disturbed at the scene. At this time the body still felt warm.

The body was thereafter removed to the mortuary in Limerick Regional Hospital for full examination.

Clothing

Red sleeveless T-shirt which was pulled up exposing the abdomen. There was a black band across the front bearing silver stars. There was no evidence of damage or significant bloodstaining.

Black cotton trousers, buttoned and zipped up

although the trousers themselves were not fully pulled up to her waist. There was bloodstaining in the crotch and over the front of the left thigh. There was also some blood over the buttocks. She was not wearing any undergarments or shoes.

Marks and injuries

The main injuries were to the neck area. There was a ligature mark around the neck and there was evidence of asphyxial signs above the ligature mark. The other significant site of injury was to the perineum (area between the rectum and the genitals) where there were injuries to the vagina and rectum, consistent with a violent sexual assault.

Dr Cassidy's postmortem conclusions revealed the full extent of the horrendous murder of an unsuspecting and innocent young woman at the hands of a boyfriend who possessed all the characteristics of the worst form of sexual psychopathic behaviour.

Conclusions

1. Postmortem examination showed that this girl died from asphyxia.
2. There was a ligature mark around the neck and petechial, or pinpoint haemorrhages,

into the skin and soft tissues of the face due to compression of the neck structures.

3. The mark was ill defined, but encircled the neck and was widest just below the left ear. This would suggest the ligature used was fairly narrow and had been held tight around her neck, the ends of the ligature possibly held just below the left ear. The lack of damage to the surface of the skin would suggest that the ligature used was not only narrow but had a fairly smooth surface.

4. The other significant injury was to the perineum. There was a large vaginal tear, extensive bruising and abrasion around the entrance to the vagina and some bruising around the anal margin. This is a clear indication of sexual assault, with violent penetration of the vagina and attempted penetration of the anus.

5. The extent of damage around the entrance to the vagina would suggest that the injuries were not due to penile penetration alone but that some object had been used. It would be difficult to determine how many times the object was inserted but certainly it was inserted with sufficient force to tear the vaginal wall, causing extensive bleeding into the soft tissues lining the inside of the pelvis.

6. The sexual assault most likely occurred when she was already unconscious, at or about the time of her death, as the vaginal injuries produced would have been extremely painful. If she had been conscious she would have been expected to struggle and resist and therefore would have shown more evidence of physical assault or restraint.

7. As she was clothed when found, and in particular her trousers were on and fastened, this would suggest that she had been re-dressed by her assailant following the assault as she would be unlikely to be in any condition to dress herself after sustaining the injuries.

8. Severe vaginal injuries of this extent have been known to cause collapse and death of an individual, even in the absence of other significant injuries. However, there is clear evidence that this girl had been asphyxiated due to ligature strangulation and was most likely already unconscious and near the point of death, if not already dead, when sexually assaulted. However the presence of such an injury to the perineum could certainly have hastened death.

9. There is no evidence to suggest that she had

been physically assaulted in any other way. Apart from a bruise on the left side of the scalp there was no evidence of any significant injuries and this minor head injury could have been caused when her upper body was being moved, as could have the few injuries around the upper arm which could have been caused when her body was being dragged after death.

10. The pubic area appears to have been shaved after death, there being no vital reaction to the shaving cuts. Cut hairs were still present on the surface of the skin, but were not found in the vagina, confirming the shaving occurred after the sexual assault.

11. There was no evidence of any naturally occurring disease which would have caused or contributed to her death.

Cause of Death

a. Asphyxia due to:

b. Ligature strangulation.

Contributory Cause: Vaginal laceration.

The family had no idea what had happened to Lorraine, other than she had been murdered. The horrible realisation that her body had lain in the flat from Sunday morning until Tuesday evening occupied and haunted their thoughts. Later on Wednesday evening members of the family including Derrick, his uncle Tom O'Connor and cousin Raymond O'Connor travelled to the mortuary of Limerick Regional Hospital.

'It was just one more devastating blow to deal with,' says Derrick. We all stood there frozen to the spot by a sight that we never thought we would see, our sister, niece and cousin lying there dead on a cold steel slab. There was weeping and crying and hugging and kissing of Lorraine. It was a sight that will stay with me for the rest of my life and the scent in the holding area.'

When it was released on Thursday the family took Lorraine's body home for a two-day wake. They experienced a gamut of emotion: shock, sadness, emptiness, regret, anger and guilt. And the cloying pain of a living nightmare. Ann was haunted by the fact that she and her family had never spotted anything in Hogan to suggest that he might be capable of killing their only daughter.

On Saturday morning October 27, 2001, Lorraine O'Connor, at the tender age of nineteen, was laid to rest in Drumcliff cemetery. A Sleeping Beauty who would never waken.

That very evening Noel Hogan, who had fled to London on an Aer Lingus flight after abandoning Ann O'Connor's car, contacted Ennis Garda station from a phone box in Paddington offering to give himself up. He was told to go to the nearest Metropolitan Police station and stay there until murder investigators arrived from Ennis to take him back.

Despite having taken over €4,000 from the safe in McCarthy's pub the previous Sunday, Hogan was broke. Clearly, he had a very good time before deciding to face the music. He was brought back to Shannon accompanied by detectives and then to Ennis Garda station where he was charged with the murder. Under questioning he admitted the charge but, like all psychopaths, his statement was a combination of fact and fantasy.

He claimed that after Seamus Ball left the flat in the early hours of Sunday morning, he and Lorraine had made love. He then told her he wanted anal sex but she refused. This led to a rage in which he grabbed a PlayStation cord and strangled her. When further pressed about the reason for the murder, he said that he wanted 'to see what it was like'. Presumably that meant he wanted to experience the 'buzz' of killing someone.

He offered to write a letter of apology to the family, which he did, but of course this gesture was entirely self-serving. Sexual psychopaths of his kind do not have one ounce of remorse for their victims, but rather often blame them for their heinous acts. Lorraine would not engage in anal sex, so was responsible for his rage. Hogan's account is not true, however, because, unlike this perverted killer, forensic science does not lie.

If he was telling the truth, there would have been a struggle. Dr Cassidy's report concludes that there were no defensive wounds on Lorraine's body indicating that the victim was taken by surprise from behind and had no opportunity to defend herself. What is far more likely is that Hogan was hatching this foul act in his mind for some time before.

What the O'Connor family did not know until later was that Hogan, like Ian Huntley, had a history of violence towards women. He had a previous conviction for assault against a woman in Tralee. His predilection for developing relations with teenage girls had resulted in the violent rape of a fourteen-year-old girl in Limerick some years before, after which he had gone on the run in England. At the time of his relationship with Lorraine, he was still wanted for that offence. Hogan had also been questioned by gardaí during an investigation into the murder of a Belgian national in a hostel where Hogan worked as a caretaker. Had his name been entered into the computer it would have thrown up the fact that he was wanted for rape.

Also unknown to the family, was that Hogan had been pressurising Lorraine to experiment with ecstasy in order to make her engage in his perverted sexual acts. Several times she had woken up while Hogan was trying to put the drug into her mouth. One time she woke up to find him masturbating over her. She confided to friends that she was so worried by this behaviour that she was seriously considering breaking up with him.

One thing Hogan and his kind react very badly to is rejection of any kind and, if Lorraine had intimated her feelings, it would have spurred his compulsion to assault and violate her. It is quite likely that he saw the comforts provided by the O'Connor family beginning to disappear. But first he would take the ultimate revenge.

There is further evidence that the time and day of the murder had a strong element of planning. Hogan had played the sheep so effectively within the family that he had been given access to the keys of the safe. He also knew that the weekend takings were kept in the O'Connor's house before being banked on the Monday.

What is more likely than his version of events is that, after the departure of Seamus Ball on Sunday morning, Hogan went into another room where he acquired the PlayStation cable and waited until Lorraine fell asleep lying on her stomach.

Clutching the cable he entered the room with a savage plan, fuelled by the evil fantasies in his mind. He went to the bed and, straddling the sleeping form of his girlfriend, slipped the cable around her neck before applying ferocious pressure. Even if Lorraine had become aware of that pressure, she would have slipped into unconsciousness within a minute and been oblivious to the events that were to follow.

Her struggle was swift and short and she was brain dead within five minutes of the oxygen deprivation. The monster Hogan could then realise his sexual fantasies in the manner of the world's worst serial killers, without resistance. He could now exercise what he wanted all his ghastly life: complete control.

He turned the prone body of his girlfriend over and raped her violently. This was followed by an attempted anal rape.

But Hogan was not successful, because many sexual psychopaths suffer from erectile dysfunction, a fact that inclines them towards violence and violation. In their evil mindset, they again blame their victim for their own inadequacies.

One would have thought that such an orgy of violence and what amounted to necrophilia would have sated the disgusting inclinations of this beast. But no, and it is a measure of his danger to women and society that Hogan further defiled his victim by attacking the genitalia with what he claimed in his statement was a Smirnoff Ice bottle.

His revolting action was redolent of the modus operandi of America's most notorious serial killer Ted Bundy who defiled the genitalia of his victims in an orgy of rage and frustration against females.

Hogan's attack, according to Dr Cassidy, would have been sufficient to cause a hugely traumatic and painful demise but thankfully, as evidenced by the strangulation and the relatively small blood loss, Lorraine would have felt nothing. If her heart had been beating there would have been considerably more blood at the scene.

It did not stop Hogan smearing what blood there was over the chest, stomach and back of his victim and then taking a razor and shaving the pubic hair to no purpose but his own sick gratification. He then dressed Lorraine and dragged her to the room where he hid her body in the base of the bed to give himself time to make good his escape.

There is no way, according to experts, that any of Hogan's

actions were either opportunistic or spontaneous. Everything about that night of horror may seem beyond belief but was initially a fantasy which was then planned right down to the last detail. Just like Ian Huntley's abduction and murder of Holly Wells and Jessica Chapman.

Does the life sentence that Noel Hogan received guarantee that this serial killer in the making will be locked up for that time? No it does not. It is discretionary, which it should not be. Readers who watch *Forensic Detectives* or *The FBI Files* on Discovery Channel will be familiar with the phrase 'life without the possibility of parole'. This is what Hogan deserves but the greatest fear that Lorraine O'Connor's family has is that he will walk the streets again.

Killers of the ilk of Hogan are highly manipulative and are able to convince naïve professionals that they are capable of rehabilitation and should be given a chance. This is not fanciful speculation as we have seen in the case of Thomas Murray who convinced the Sentence Review Group he could be let out on temporary release. Nancy Nolan paid for this error with her life.

Don't imagine that the killer of Lorraine O'Connor is not capable of doing the same again. Like Huntley, Hogan was on the run from one violent rape and is suspected to have been involved in another unsolved attack. The O'Connor family justifiably feel that they were let down by the system. The last morsel of peace they may be allowed is the knowledge that the foul killer of their lovely Lorraine will never be free to put another family through the same pain and unending anguish.

It is the least they deserve from a system that has already failed them.

Only then will their Sleeping Beauty also rest in peace.

On the first anniversary of their beloved's death, Lorraine's brother Derrick and his girlfriend Helen wrote this in her memory:

> *One year ago on this day my darling sister went away. I'm sending this tribute up above to Lorraine, my sister that I love. Across the skies beneath the winds to a special place where only angels sing. You are the brightest star, the whitest dove, now in the wings of Heaven's love. There's a special gift in life that's rare, it's a love that a brother and sister have shared. We've had that love, Lorraine, you and I, from the day you were born till the day you died. You may be out of sight, Lorraine, and even worlds apart, you are always on my mind and forever in my heart.*
>
> *From your loving brother,*
> *Derrick and girlfriend Helen*

And from little brother Darragh:

> *I love you and miss you. It has been a long year. I have to carry on without you. I so wish you were here. If only you could have taken your phone to Heaven, I would call you every day. I would beg you to come home and never go away.*

You were always there with a helping hand, you helped me with my homework and the things I didn't understand. I loved you then Lorraine, I love you still. Throughout my life I always will.

Your loving brother, Darragh

ALSO FROM
MICHAEL SHERIDAN

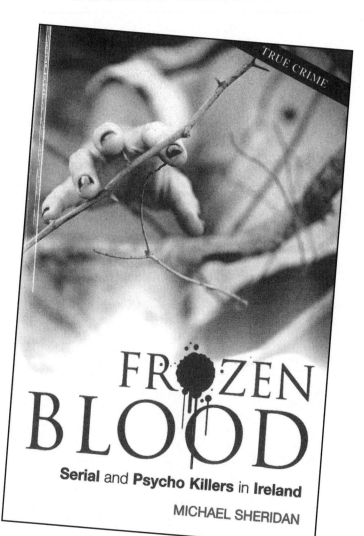

TRUE CRIME

FR⬤ZEN
BLO⬤D

Serial and **Psycho Killers** in **Ireland**

MICHAEL SHERIDAN